HOLY HABITS

Andrew Roberts

malcolm down
PUBLISHING

British Library Cataloguing in Publication Data

A catalogue record for this book is available from the British Library

ISBN 978-1910786-15-4

Cover Image © Juliet Hemingray Church Textiles
Cover Design: Esther Kotecha
Back page photograph courtesy of BowlandMedia.
Printed in the UK by Bell & Bain Ltd, Glasgow

What Others Are Saying...

Holy Habits is about the heart of the Christian life – about being shaped by Jesus Christ as we follow him. Andrew writes simply and compellingly from his own experience as a church leader and pioneer, and most of all as a human being seeking to know and share God's love. He takes the rich traditions of Christian discipline and translates them into language that anyone can access and put into practice. His book will help you find holiness. I commend it warmly.
Paul Bayes, Bishop of Liverpool

Grounded in practice and real-life stories and surrounded by theory, erudition and wide reading, this is one of the best books I've read on discipleship. The examples come from all round the world, from different sources, from fresh expressions[1] and traditional Christians, from elderly people and young ones, women as well as men. I love the way the habits are every day, ordinary, do-able ones. This feels very godly.
Lucy Moore, Messy Church

Just the job! An accessible and authentic account of Christian discipleship, full of encouragement and insight. Which, when linked with the material on Holy Habits becomes a resource for Christian fruitfulness for each and every small group and local congregation I can think of.
Martyn Atkins, Team Leader and Superintendent Minister, Methodist Central Hall, Westminster

In *Holy Habits* Andrew Roberts has created an excellent manual for discipleship in the way of Jesus. Drawing on the practices of the early church, insights from current practitioners, a host of great stories and his own wide experience, Andrew has distilled the life of discipleship into ten 'Holy Habits'. He is never prescriptive, rather inviting the reader to work with the principle of each holy habit in their own context and tradition. Holy Habits will be transformative reading for individuals, churches, fresh expressions and for anyone who hopes to see the world reshaped/transfigured in the way of Jesus. *Holy Habits* will leave you imagining, praying and working for a better world now. I am delighted to commend *Holy Habits*.

Ian Adams, poet, author, pioneer and priest

In our busy, bustling lives it can be difficult to make room for God. In this book, Andrew goes back to basics – to the very beginning of the early church – and discovers the hidden treasures of practices which encourage readers to develop a rhythm and pattern to their life and discipleship. Andrew offers biblical reflection alongside real-life stories of transformation which have happened to some ordinary and many extraordinary followers of Jesus. This is a book for anyone trying to work out their faith in messy lives. It is a book for those who want to go deeper in their understanding and practice of their faith. It is also a book for those who are stagnant or stuck and want to be challenged or try out something different.

Joanne Cox-Darling, Methodist Presbyter, author and Learning and Development Co-ordinator

Holy Habits contains deep reflection, wide experience of the church, theology and new expressions of mission and service. It is full of captivating illustrations and practical ways forward for the reader. Each chapter asks challenging questions personally, locally and globally.

Howard Mellor, Senior Minister, Methodist International Church, Hong Kong

Many books on discipleship seem to focus on process rather than habit. In this book Andrew Roberts suggests simple lifestyle changes for individuals and groups, which add up to 'Jesus living' with impact. No need to go on conferences, do courses or enrol for a course in theology.

Just read this, put it into practice and be amazed at the difference true discipleship can make.
Norman Ivison, Director of Communications, Fresh Expressions

Andrew Roberts' easy-going style is accessible to anyone exploring discipleship in the busyness of the twenty-first century. His faith shines through every chapter, and his multiple real-life stories keep the message grounded in reality. Reflections, challenges and suggested actions are gifts for individuals and small-groups – a blessing for churches that are serious about creating deeper connections with their community.
Linda Rayner, United Reformed Church, Co-ordinator for Fresh Expressions

The joy of this immensely readable book is that it will help those who are new to the Christian journey to develop practices that will nurture their spiritual formation and it will help those who are a bit further along the road to sustain it.
Ian Bell, Pioneer Ministries Coordinator (Venture FX and Methodist Pioneering Pathways)

Endnotes

1. Throughout this book 'Fresh Expressions' (initial caps) denotes the Ecumenical Agency set up to support the formation of new ecclesial communities and the movement it has encouraged, while 'fresh expressions' (lower case) is used for the new ecclesial communities themselves.

Contents

Acknowledgements

I have been journeying with the idea of holy habits for several years now. My journey began in Durham when I wrote an essay on Acts 2 as part of an MA in Theology for which I studied at Cranmer Hall/Wesley Study Centre. There I was encouraged by the likes of Mark Bonnington, Steven Croft, Anne Dyer, Gavin Wakefield, Roger Walton and David Wilkinson. The essay was subsequently rewritten and published in the *Epworth Review*. The next step in the development of the concept came when I rewrote the Fresh Expressions' *mission shaped ministry* course module on discipleship. It was then that I first used the phrase 'holy habits' in relation to the discipleship practices we see in Acts 2. The idea of writing a book slowly began to form and then a sabbatical began to appear on the horizon. An ideal time to get down to some writing.

Another significant moment came when I was invited to support a strategic review conducted by the Birmingham Methodist Circuit. The review identified a need to deepen discipleship within the Circuit and its constituent churches. Together with Reverend Deborah Humphries and Circuit Treasurer Brian Dickens I was asked to develop some ideas as to how deeper discipleship could be nurtured. Amidst a fruitful conversation I suggested developing a programme around the ten holy habits. The idea was warmly received and the Circuit wholeheartedly began work on producing a programme under the excellent leadership of Superintendent Neil Johnson and a superb team of Caz Hague, Deborah Humphries, Michele Simms, Rachel Frank, Tom Milton and Vicki Atkinson. I have been privileged to be part of that team. The *Holy Habits* programme was launched at the International Conference Centre, Birmingham in May 2015. The programme is proving to be an inspiration. This book is an independent project but one that closely complements the programme.

I would like to thank the Methodist Church for the gift of a sabbatical during which most of the book was written. I would also like to thank my colleagues and friends Caroline, Geoff, Inderjit, Liam, Bill, Jemima and Steve who covered some of my regular duties whilst I was on sabbatical.

Ian Adams, Martyn Atkins, Paul Bayes, Ian Bell, Ben Clymo, Joanne Cox-Darling, Alison Craggs, Olive Fleming-Drane, Lynne Hunt, Norman Ivison, Howard Mellor, Lucy Moore, Linda Rayner, Shona Roberts and Roger Walton have all kindly reviewed the drafts of the book. Thank you all very much for your wisdom, insights, encouragement and theological grit which have all helped to improve the early drafts. Any remaining shortcomings are entirely my responsibility.

Special thanks to my publisher Malcolm Down and his team including Esther Kotecha, Sarah Griggs and Louise Stenhouse. Malcolm and I grew up together and were blessed to be part of a vibrant fellowship at Berkswich Methodist Church, Stafford which greatly encouraged us in our following of Jesus.

Thanks are also due to Juliet Hemingray. Back in the 90s she provided me with the outfit in which I made my modelling debut as part of Clergy on the Catwalk, ending up on the front page of the *Independent* newspaper and in the 'And finally . . .' item on *News at Ten*. This time around she kindly provided the cover image for the book.

To the many people who have supported me on my own adventure of discipleship I say thank you. There are so many who have played a part in this and I am grateful to every one of you but rather than risking forgetting someone please accept my thanks to you all.

This book is dedicated to my lovely wife Shona and my wonderful son Matthew. For your love, support and toleration of my appetite for *Sky Sports* I am deeply grateful.

Preface

Follow me![1] The adventure began with these two simple yet life-changing, world-changing words. Ordinary people in the midst of their everyday lives were captivated by the person of Jesus and set out on a journey that would change both them and the course of human history.

So just in case you were wondering, *Holy Habits* is a book about following Jesus, about Christian discipleship. It is a not a clothing catalogue for nuns.

The call of Jesus to discipleship rang clear on the shores of Lake Galilee. Around the world millions of people are still hearing that call and setting out on the adventure of Christian discipleship. But what does that look like, involve and mean in the unfolding twenty-first century?

In *Holy Habits* we will explore the call of Jesus to discipleship today. We will consider how disciples are formed. We will examine a number of key biblical texts. We will reflect upon the themes of adventure and suffering. We will explore the place of community and holy habits in forming and sustaining Christian disciples. And we will dare to suggest how the world could experience more wholesome transformation and healing if there were more effective disciples of Jesus.

This book is not about religiosity. It is not about an abstract piety. And it is definitely not about a narcissistic 'bless me' spirituality. Rather it is about a divinely inspired and infused wholesome humanity that seeks to live generously and graciously in harmony with God and the whole of creation. It is a 24/7 calling and a Kingdom calling to be worked out in every facet of our lives: our relationships and our sense of self; our work and our leisure; our care of creation and our struggle for justice.

The book is in two parts. Part One explores the nature of discipleship and has five chapters.

1. The Adventure of Discipleship.
2. The Adventure Begins – which includes an exploration of the call narratives in the Gospels.
3. The Aims of Discipleship.
4. Suffering and the Sacrificial Nature of Discipleship.
5. Signs and Wonders.

Part Two explores the nurture of discipleship beginning with a chapter on holy habitats before a chapter on each of the holy habits that we see in the first Christian community described by Luke in Acts 2. The ten habits are:

- Biblical teaching
- Fellowship
- Breaking of bread
- Prayer
- Giving
- Service
- Eating together
- Gladness and generosity
- Worship
- Making more disciples

At the end of each chapter there are suggestions for further reflection and action that can be used individually or by smaller or larger Christian communities. I have also included a biblical passage to reflect upon and suggestions for further reading. The suggested books are drawn from a wide variety of sources and theological perspectives. Some of these may fit your preferences whilst others you may find more stretching or challenging. There is a full and detailed bibliography at the end of the book.

A final chapter invites you to dare to dream. To imagine what your home, your community, your workplace, your church and the wider world could be like if the holy habits were lived fully and enthusiastically, fired by the Spirit and centred on the Holy Community of the Trinity.

I write this book as a disciple of Jesus. The root meaning of the Greek word for disciple, *mathetes*, is 'one who learns as they follow'. I identify with that meaning and write as one who is learning as I seek to follow, recognising that I still have much to learn.

When it comes to discipleship there are few experts and even fewer, if any, perfect exponents. Personally I am a million miles away from the wisdom and holiness of people on whose wisdom and writings I have drawn such as David Watson, Sheila Cassidy, Dietrich Bonhoeffer, Lucy Moore and Ian Adams. I am equally far away from the godliness and virtue of saints such as Joy who you will meet in Chapter 4. I am not worthy to untie the sandals of the biblical scholars that are referenced in this book. And when it comes to adventure I am definitely no Bear Grylls or Bono!

So I write in humility, fully aware that there will be weaknesses and shortcomings in what I offer but with the hope and prayer that *Holy Habits* will help you in your following of Jesus at home, at work, in the community and as part of the company of disciples called church. I also offer the book to help those who are seeking to form or grow communities of faith and belonging – churches – that aim to develop fruitful disciples of Jesus at this intriguing and challenging time in human history. This aim is central to the life and mission of the church. As Martyn Atkins commented: 'Any "Church", inherited, emerging or whatever, is not fulfilling a basic function of "Church" if it is not enabling disciples of Christ to be made and deeper disciples of Christ to emerge. This is the acid test of Church.'[2]

Endnotes

1. Mark 1:17; Matthew 4:19.

2. Quote taken from the Fresh Expressions *mission shaped ministry course* unit B04 Discipleship Teachers Notes, p6.

Part 1
The Nature of Discipleship

1
The Adventure of Discipleship

Jesus said to Simon, 'Don't be afraid; from now on you will fish for people.' So they pulled their boats up on shore, left everything and followed him.
Luke 5:10b–11 NIV

The adventure of Christian discipleship begins with the call of Jesus to follow. As disciples we may be more or less clear or confused as to who Jesus is and what following him means. We may or may not have consciously encountered Jesus previously or thought of him before. The call may come loudly or quietly, instantaneously or gradually, but 'the initiative is with Jesus'.[1] It is he who invites us to share his life, his mission and his sufferings. When we respond to that invitation we don't know where the journey will take us.

A Journey into the Unknown
Since embarking on the adventure of discipleship as a teenager my following of Jesus has led me to study economics at the University

of York, to work as a financial analyst with Ford Motor Company and to service as a minister in the Methodist Church. I have lived in Basildon, Durham, Doncaster and Dudley. For eight years I worked for the ecumenical Fresh Expressions team being privileged to see God birthing all manner of new Christian communities and helping to train those leading them. With the Fresh Expressions team I travelled all over the UK from Aberdeen to Penzance and even went to Barbados (I know but someone had to go).

I have been blessed with a beautiful wife and a fabulous son. I have survived two serious car crashes, badly broken my arm, watched my dad slowly and partially recover from a massive stroke and my mum care for him. I have carried the coffin of a baby and told a father that his son had hanged himself. I have been privileged to share all manner of celebrations and to hold those grieving and hurting. I have planted churches and pastored churches. I have had the great joy of seeing people come to faith in Jesus and baptised many. I have been humbled to meet some amazing saints of God – extraordinary, ordinary people, some of whom I will introduce you to later on. I have also experienced the deep sadness of churches putting people off Jesus.

I have been to Live Aid and the Olympic Games and seen all manner of great artists perform including Michael Jackson, U2 and Beyoncé. I had my own fifteen minutes of fame appearing on the front page of the *Independent* newspaper and on seventeen TV channels when I headlined the first 'Clergy on the Catwalk' show, following that up by appearing on the BBC's *Get Your Own Back* dressed as a dog, a flower and a rotund chef. I have also won the only stock car race held exclusively for pastors, preachers and vicars.

I have been loved a lot and lied to. Helped and hurt. Achieved a fair bit and failed many times. Got some things right and many things wrong.

Why do I share all this? Because this is how it is when we commit to following Jesus. We don't know where the adventure will lead. I had no idea that the experiences I have listed and many more that I could, but won't, bore you with would come my way when I committed to following Jesus as a teenager. But what I have known all the way is the faithfulness of the one who calls us and says to us as he says to his first disciples, 'I am with you always.'[2]

At the U2 gig I went to Bono, bearing witness to his commitment to Jesus, spoke to the heart of the wonder and mystery of the adventure of following Jesus when he said, 'We don't know where we are going, but we know who we are going with.'[3]

Learning As We Follow

The Greek New Testament word translated into English as 'disciple' is *mathetes*. It is often said to mean either a follower or a learner. The literal meaning is 'one who learns as they follow'. So the primary activity of discipleship is following with the learning happening as the adventure of following unfolds, helping to shape and guide the unfolding journey. As the biblical commentator Raymond Brown points out 'follow is the term par excellence for the dedication of discipleship'.[4] Roger Walton in his excellent book *Disciples Together* puts it this way: 'to be a disciple is to hear the call of Jesus, to take up that call and follow him, to let go of everything to engage in God's mission and be transformed in the process'.[5]

This primacy of following is important as it points us to an active, lived-out discipleship and warns us against a faith that is merely abstract or theoretical. Just as I can read every book on motoring and know all the theory but could not call myself a motorist until I get in the driver's seat, engage first gear and start driving, so I cannot claim to be a disciple of Jesus if I read all the books, know all the theory but do not actively follow the one I claim to be the disciple of.

The calling is personal and relational. Jesus calls us to follow *him*. Not a philosophy or a set of ideas, far less a long list of rules or regulations. The call to Christian discipleship is a call to follow the inspiring, challenging, occasionally enigmatic but above all and always, loving one, called Jesus Christ, the Son of God.[6]

In her book *The Disciple* Lucy Peppiatt puts it this way:

Jesus calls us to follow him, and in this means following where he leads. It means 'following' in so many different ways. We follow him like we follow a dance partner. We follow his teachings. We follow the leading of the Spirit. We follow in his footsteps to the cross. We follow his example in loving the outcast, praying for the sick, and delivering those who are oppressed by demons. We follow him because he has won us: by his love and his beauty, his power and grace, his truth and forgiveness.[7]

A Journey for All

In understanding discipleship as an adventure it's important to note that active and adventurous are not necessarily physical attributes. Those limited by age or disability can be *very* active and adventurous in their following of Jesus: spiritually, imaginatively and particularly prayerfully. In fact when it comes to the holy habits of discipleship there are many inspiring examples of practitioners of the habits who are energised by the Spirit in ways that more than overcome any limitations of age or physical ability.

As a young Christian at University I, with a few others students, was adopted by a retired postman called Les. Les was a delightful cocktail of a Christian. A faithful Methodist local preacher of many years' service, he was also very much at home in the newly forming charismatic house churches in York. At a time when Les could easily have put his feet up, he made it his mission to support those many years younger than him embarking on the adventure of discipleship. Every week he would slip the bike clips around his trouser legs and ride his shaky bike up the hill to the university where he would meet with us and pray for us. Then we in turn would go to his flat to read the Bible and eat together – sandwiches so big you almost needed to dislocate your jaw to eat them washed down by huge mugs of Yorkshire tea. Simply sharing the holy habits of discipleship Les helped to inspire a new generation of followers of Jesus.

An Urgent Spirit-filled Adventure

At the time Jesus walked this earth there were lots of people who would claim an allegiance of discipleship to those they were following and learning from. There were plenty of rabbis and others who were offering their particular understanding and experience of discipleship to those willing to follow their teachings. Conventional rabbinic discipleship in the early years of the first century AD was focused on learning the law or will of God (Torah) as revealed in the first five books of the Old Testament (the Pentateuch) and the Prophets. So what was distinctive about Jesus' call to discipleship?

Discipleship for the followers of Jesus was a matter of sharing his life, ministry and mission. Learning happened both on the go and in community. With Jesus there was a shift in emphasis from the past to the present – being aware of what God is doing now – and to the future for the 'the kingdom of God has come near'.[8] According to renowned Scottish theologian James Dunn, the call of Jesus to discipleship and the relationship between Jesus and his disciples were distinguished by their 'charismatic – eschatological'[9] nature. These are big theological words that may be off-putting to some, either because they are big or because they may be thought to only apply to particular groups of followers of Jesus.

The word 'charismatic' means different things to different people. In popular everyday usage bright, inspiring personalities are often described as charismatic. When I put the words 'charismatic personalities' into Google, images came up of Jonny Depp, Barack and Michele Obama, Oprah Winfrey, Richard Branson, Steve Jobs and Nelson Mandela. Even Margaret Thatcher and Sarah Palin appeared which, depending on your perspectives, may or may not surprise you.

For many Christians the word charismatic is most associated with ecstatic worship and the exercising of the gifts of the Spirit, particularly those listed by Paul in 1 Corinthians 12. For Dunn the essence of the charismatic nature of Jesus and his first followers was a godly power and authority.[10] Others would point to the root meaning of the word charismatic derived from two Greek words: *charis*, meaning grace and *mata* meaning gifts. Taking this understanding, charismatic people and communities are marked by generosity and giving. I like to be a both/and person and suggest there is value in blending all of these understandings when reflecting on how disciples of Jesus should be, both individually and collectively. Attractive in personality, inspiring, imbued with a godly power and authority and full of the holy habits of graciousness and generosity.

In contrast to charismatic, eschatological is not a word used on *X-Factor, The Voice* or even *Daily Politics*. It is a technical theological term referring to the end times (the eschaton) when the reign of God will be apparent. Jesus spoke and lived in a way that explained and demonstrated that the Kingdom of God was a present as well as a future reality. For the first Christian disciples that which the prophets of the Hebrew Bible and the people of God prior to the birth of Jesus had longed for was at hand, breaking into the here and now. It was a *realised* eschatology. This was good news and a spur to urgent action. For the first followers of Jesus there was a palpable sense of excitement and urgency not least because they were on edge with anticipation that the Lord would return soon. They did not expect the eschatological age to last long which gave an urgency to their life as a community and their missional activity.

With the passing of 2000 years or so the sense of urgency and eschatological fervour has faded amongst Western Christians. This is understandable but it also presents a challenge. A challenge to rediscover a healthy sense of passion and adventure in responding to Jesus' call to follow without at the same time falling into the trap of disappearing down some cultic cul-de-sac predicting that Jesus will return next Tuesday.

We live in a needy and dangerous age. As I write this the news is full of stories of extreme violence, of people fleeing their lands taking extraordinary risks to find a new home, and of Western nations continuing to flirt with economic bankruptcy. The spectre of climate change casts a dark shadow and there are still enough weapons in the world to blow it up many times over. It is against this background that the call of Jesus comes. For many hearing that call in Africa, Asia, the Middle East and Latin America the sense of eschatological urgency experienced by the first followers of Jesus is still alive and real. Their experiences are a challenge to those of us who live in apparently more comfortable and less threatening situations. A challenge to prayer and action, and a warning against complacency.

Struggle on the Way

In the midst of the urgent it is also important to remember that all adventures have their times of fatigue, struggle, dullness and doubt as well as their times of discovery, excitement, energy and wonder. In Chapter 4 we will reflect more on the place of struggle and suffering. The great adventurer Bear Grylls said this about following Jesus:

> When we pursue an adventurous path through life, inevitably we are going to have moments of hardship, doubt, struggle and pain. It goes with the territory. But for me, my simple faith has so often brought light to a dark path, joy to a cold mountain and strength to a failing body. Believing doesn't mean we have to suddenly get all religious. I am not. And Jesus certainly wasn't. It has taken a while in my life to understand that faith is a journey, and as we trust and lean on Him, He leads us to the light – to a freer, more centred existence, free from guilt, free from crippling fear and free to start living.[11]

Moments of hardship, doubt, struggle and pain are part of the human condition. They are also an inevitable part of the adventure of discipleship for we follow the one who says, 'If any want to become my followers, let them deny themselves and take up their cross and follow me.'[12]

Sometimes, maybe often, to be adventurous in following Jesus means being involved in very ordinary activities which nevertheless push us to the limits. For example engaging in local politics by standing up for the marginalised or asylum seekers or being involved in a movement against people-trafficking. Being the teacher who willingly takes the difficult kids, the doctor who opts to support the methadone clinic, the cleaner who keeps the toilets immaculate or the business executive who takes a pay cut so that someone else can keep their job when orders are low.

Disturb Us Lord

The need for active, adventurous disciples of Jesus is as urgent as ever. There is a broken world in need of healing, good news to be shared and Kingdom work to be done, all energised by the charismatic Spirit so powerfully present at the baptism of Jesus[13] and the birth of the church at Pentecost.[14]

The great explorer Sir Francis Drake, who knew a thing or two about adventure, made this his prayer:

Disturb us, Lord, when
We are too well pleased with ourselves,
When our dreams have come true
Because we have dreamed too little,
When we arrived safely
Because we sailed too close to the shore.
Disturb us, Lord, when
With the abundance of things we possess
We have lost our thirst
For the waters of life;
Having fallen in love with life,
We have ceased to dream of eternity
And in our efforts to build a new earth,
We have allowed our vision
Of the new Heaven to dim.
Disturb us, Lord, to dare more boldly,
To venture on wider seas
Where storms will show your mastery;
Where losing sight of land,
We shall find the stars.

We ask You to push back
The horizons of our hopes;
And to push into the future
In strength, courage, hope, and love.

Suggestions for Further Reflection and Action

Personally

Take time to reflect on the call of Jesus. How do you feel when you hear his words 'Follow me'? Excited? Confused? Nostalgic? Fearful? Energised? Find a trusted friend to talk with about your thoughts and feelings.

Who do you know who might be finding the adventure particularly challenging at this time? What support might you offer to them?

Locally

In what ways does your local Christian community, your church offer opportunities to explore the call of Jesus to follow?

Reflect on Drake's poem. One of the biblical metaphors for the church is a boat. Imagine your church as a sailing boat. Where is that boat at the moment? In the safety of the harbour? Heading out to sea? Caught in a storm? How strongly is the wind of the Spirit blowing through your sails? How could you catch a fresh wind?

Globally

Let you and your fellowship be inspired by the adventures of others following Jesus around the world. Plan an adventure in partnership with a church in another country.

Consider how you can pray for, campaign for and support those in greatest need and danger in the world at the moment. How might you be able to offer help or hospitality to those fleeing their homes and seeking refuge?

A Biblical Passage to Reflect On

• Mark 1:9–20

What do you notice in this passage?

What will you do or change in the light of what you have read and noticed?

Recommended Reading

- Steven Croft, *Jesus' People: What the Church Should Do Next*.
- Simon Guillebaud, *More Than Conquerors*.
- John Ortberg, *If You Want to Walk on Water, You've Got to Get Out of the Boat*.

Endnotes

1. Roger L. Walton, *Disciples Together*, London: SCM Press, 2014, p4.
2. Matthew 28:20.
3. If you want to explore more of Bono's journey of adventurous discipleship I would recommend Steve Stockman's book, *Walk On: The Spiritual Journey of U2*.
4. Raymond Brown, *The Gospel According to John* (Volume 1), London: Geoffrey Chapman, 1966, p78.
5. Roger L. Walton, *Disciples Together*, London: SCM Press, 2014, p6.
6. Mark 1:1.
7. Lucy Peppiatt, *The Disciple*, Eugene: Cascade, 2012.
8. Mark 1:15.
9. James D.G. Dunn, *Jesus and the Spirit*, London: SCM Press, 1975, p80.
10. Ibid, p87.
11. https://m.facebook.com/notes/bear-grylls/proud-to-read-this-tonight-at-the-carols-service-supporting-these-brave-kids-gre/10153599881040327/.
12. Matthew 16:24.
13. Mark 1:10, Matthew 3:16, Luke 3:22.
14. Acts 2:1–4.

2

The Adventure Begins

Lord your summons echoes true
when you but call my name.
Let me turn and follow you
and never be the same.
In your company I'll go
where your love and footsteps show.
Thus I'll move and live and grow
in you and you in me.
(John L. Bell and Graham Maule,
Wild Goose Resource Group)[1]

The birth story of each human person is highly significant. It can provide illuminating insights into the subsequent formation of the one who was born. So, too, can the birth stories of communities or movements. The insights we discover in their origins can tell us a great deal about the ethos or DNA of the bodies or organisations that grow from them.

For the first followers of Jesus, discipleship was active, purposeful,

Kingdom-focused and adventurous. There is a powerful sense of adventure in all the Gospel accounts of the call of Jesus to the first disciples. In all four stories there is wonder, mystery and a sense of urgency. Discipleship is exciting, challenging and revolutionary. In the midst of their ordinary lives, ordinary people are called to follow on a journey that will transform them and transform the world. So how did it all begin? In this chapter we take a look at the call narratives in the four Gospels and what they say to us about the nature of Christian discipleship. Discipleship that is nurtured by the holy habits we will explore in Part 2 of the book.

The Call to Adventure in Mark and Matthew

The accounts of the call of the first disciples are virtually identical in Mark and Matthew. They present Jesus walking by Lake Galilee. There he sees the brothers Andrew and Simon (soon to be renamed Peter) casting their nets into the sea. 'Follow me,' says Jesus and 'immediately they left their nets and followed him.'[2] As far as we know they had no idea where they were going, what they would do or how long it would all last. But there was something about the one who called them that made them go on this journey of discovery. And as if to reinforce the point both Matthew and Mark present James and John being called and responding in the same way as Andrew and Peter.

> *As Jesus passed along the Sea of Galilee, he saw Simon and his brother Andrew casting a net into the sea – for they were fishermen. And Jesus said to them, 'Follow me and I will make you fish for people.' And immediately they left their nets and followed him. As he went a little farther, he saw James son of Zebedee and his brother John, who were in their boat mending the nets. Immediately he called them; and they left their father Zebedee in the boat with the hired men, and followed him.*[3]

In Mark's call narrative the initiative is clearly with Jesus. He calls; Simon and Andrew, then James and John, follow. This contrasts with most communities of discipleship at the time when it was the would-be disciples that chose the rabbi they wanted to follow. It also presents a challenge for the making of disciples in the present-day age when choice is sacred and the emphasis is increasingly on individuals choosing the lifestyle that suits them best.

It is a moot point as to whether the lakeside episode was the first time the four had encountered Jesus. As we shall see shortly, Luke suggests it was not the first meeting, but whether it is the first or the latest in a series of encounters, there was certainly something compelling, attractive and authoritative in the charismatic character of Jesus and the call that drew the fishermen into the adventure of discipleship.

Right from the beginning of Mark's Gospel the deeply relational nature of Christian discipleship is apparent. This continues with each of the sections of Jesus' ministry in Mark.[4] They each begin with a piece about discipleship indicating the integral relationship for Mark between Jesus and those who follow him.[5] As the Gospel of John and the writings of Paul go on to make even more clear, the amazing wonder and mystery is that Christian discipleship is about more than following Jesus – it is about being in, and becoming like, the one we follow.[6]

Context of Call

The context of the call of the first disciples is significant. Andrew, Simon-Peter, James and John encounter Jesus and his call to follow in the midst of their ordinary, everyday lives. Their work is affirmed and reinterpreted by Jesus. The commentator Donald English notes that it is as Jesus 'indicates the implications of the ordinary elements of life by putting them into the context of God's purposes for their lives that they [the disciples] begin to see how much more is involved'.[7]

God can and does call people to follow and serve in places set aside for worship and at great festivals, but the call can come anywhere. For most people the primary context in which their discipleship is lived out is not the temple or the church building but the home, the workplace and the community. Too often we can neglect these contexts for the living-out of discipleship and equate discipleship with dutiful church membership and service. Even worse we can sometimes reduce the adventure to turning up, shutting up and paying up.

True discipleship is not dull. Whether we are doing our bit to serve others and care for creation like my scrap dealer friend Keith – whose carefully washed but still-oil-marked hands reaching out to receive the bread of Holy Communion always reminded me of the down-to-earth nature of discipleship – or strutting our stuff on the grand stages of international football like England International Eniola Aluko our discipleship is lived out everywhere. In an interview with the BBC Eniola said this about her lived-out faith:

> I've grown up believing in God and I believe that being an England international and a lawyer has not just happened by accident. I'm a person who has a relationship with God, and it's a very active one. So whether I'm having my breakfast, driving, stood on the pitch or about to take a penalty, I will be praying, or in my mind speaking to God.[8]

Urgency

In keeping with the thoughts about urgency in Chapter 1, there is an urgency in Mark's account of the calling of the first disciples. The word *immediately* appears twice. No messing about, the adventure begins. Straight away they are given missional purpose by Jesus. From now on they will 'fish for people'. Discipleship is outward looking, Kingdom focused.

We noted in Chapter 1 how we live in a needy and dangerous age. There are many needs that need urgent responses. Violence, climate change, the abuse of women and children, economic instability, to name just a few. And in the midst of these challenges there is the continuing call of Jesus to make more disciples.[9] The sense of urgency that we find in the call narratives of all four Gospels challenges us to active, adventurous discipleship.

This urgency and the trust that Jesus invested in the first novice disciples presents us with another challenge. How willing are we to involve, challenge and trust those new to journeying with Jesus? Thankfully there are many Christian communities, churches and organisations that are willing to encourage, empower and support younger people and those of any age who are new to Christian discipleship – and significantly these are often the groups that are the most missionally active and growing. But there are others where it seems people have to wait for ever to be trusted with responsibility or leadership. Jesus got his disciples involved straight away. He trained them on the job. They had little if any prior experience, no formal qualifications and just three years with Jesus before his death, resurrection and ascension.

Community

We saw earlier how the initiative is with Jesus when it comes to Christian discipleship. He calls, we follow and this is now deeply counter-cultural in a highly self-centred, consumerist world. In a further challenge to individualism it is important to note that the first disciples were called together and into community. A community that would become known as church. As Alison Morgan helpfully reminds us in the title of her latest book, the plural of disciple is church.[10]

It's very likely that as fellow fishermen, Andrew, Simon-Peter, James and John would have known each other. Much less likely that the first four disciples would have known the other eight that Jesus called to be community with him. A reminder to us that when we respond to the call of Jesus to follow we can't be too choosy about who we journey with.

Cost

The final point to note from Mark is the way in which he emphasises the cost and sacrificial nature of discipleship – something we will explore more fully in Chapter 4.

Andrew and Simon-Peter, and James and John leave their nets to follow. There is no evidence that they did so permanently. But even if (as is entirely possible) they returned to their boats at regular intervals and used their businesses to support the travelling ministry of Jesus, there was still a personal cost in embarking on the adventure of discipleship. And that cost was emotional and relational as well as financial. We are left to wonder how James and John felt when they left their father and friends and how they in turn felt when they saw the two brothers heading off with this charismatic character called Jesus.

The Call to Adventure in Luke

Luke's first call narrative contains many elements of Mark's and Matthew's accounts, adding the story of the miraculous catch of fish.[11]

Once while Jesus was standing beside the lake of Gennesaret, and the crowd was pressing in on him to hear the word of God, he saw two boats there at the shore of the lake; the fishermen had gone out of them and were washing their nets. He got into one of the boats, the one belonging to Simon, and asked him to put out a little way from the shore. Then he sat down and taught the crowds from the boat. When he had finished speaking, he said to Simon, 'Put out into the deep water and let down your nets for a catch.' Simon answered, 'Master, we have worked all night long but have caught nothing. Yet if you say so, I will let down the nets.' When they had done this, they caught so many fish that their nets were beginning to break. So they signalled their partners in the other boat to come and help them. And they came and filled both boats, so that they began to sink. But when Simon Peter saw it, he fell down at Jesus' knees, saying, 'Go away from me, Lord, for I am a sinful man!' For he and all who were with him were amazed at the catch of fish that they had taken; and so also were James and John, sons of Zebedee, who were partners with Simon. Then Jesus said to Simon, 'Do not be afraid; from now on you will be catching people.' When they had brought their boats to shore, they left everything and followed him.[12]

Luke's call account comes in the context of people listening to the word of God. He doesn't tell us explicitly that Simon, James and John were actively listening along with the crowds but it is safe to assume they had at least a general awareness of what was going on. And it is *highly* likely that when Jesus sat in Simon's boat to teach that he was paying attention.

In the search for fresh ways of deepening discipleship we need to be careful that we don't neglect the core disciplines or holy habits that have been critical to discipleship formation and growth ever since Jesus walked this earth. One of these is listening to, engaging with and being formed by God's word, a habit we will explore more fully in Chapter 8 when we look at biblical teaching.

Challenge

Right at the beginning of his journey of discipleship Simon is presented with a challenge by Jesus: 'Put out into deep water, and let down the nets for a catch.' Responding to and overcoming challenges can be a source of growth in so many aspects of life. It is easy to succumb to the temptation of avoiding challenge. We're too young or too old. We don't have enough experience. It's too risky. This episode reminds us again of the value of challenge in growing disciples. Jesus was not slow in challenging Simon Peter and his companions to go beyond their experience and comfort zones, thereby helping them to grow in confidence. Are we sometimes too cautious? In encouraging others in their discipleship could we be more challenging?

> When I was learning to swim I was taking forever, sticking to the shallow end, keeping my inflatable arm bands on, and going nowhere. Until one day when my previously oh-so-patient instructor took off the arm bands and threw me in the deep end. And guess what? I found I could swim.

Now I am *not* advocating this as an approach for swimming teachers (it would break all Health and Safety and Safeguarding rules) but I share this story to say that sometimes in our discipleship there will be those moments when we are called to go beyond our comfort zones and discover God's resources in new ways. And there will also be times when we will need to encourage others to take steps of faith on the adventure of discipleship.

To his credit Simon did respond to the challenge he was set.
Simon answered, 'Master, we've worked hard all night and haven't caught anything. But because you say so, I will let down the nets.'

I'd love to be able to hear Simon's tone at this point. Did he say 'because you say so' with excitement and enthusiasm or with sullen, cynical or grumpy Jack Dee (or Eeyore) like tones. Discipleship maybe an adventure but there will be days when we are more enthusiastic about it and others when we would rather do the spiritual equivalent of snuggling back under the duvet.

Miraculous Freedom

Simon was set free to start living in a new way that day on Lake Galilee.[13] His call came in the context of hearing the word of God, in the midst of his everyday life, and it also began with a miracle. Luke is not shy when it comes to the place of miracles. His Gospel and Acts are full of the miraculous.[14] Biblical commentator Howard Marshall points out 'Luke's story shows that the call took place only after the fishermen had made the acquaintance of Jesus and experienced a revelation of his divine power'.[15] In the chronology of Luke's Gospel Simon had already encountered the power of Jesus when his mother-in-law was healed.[16]

As Simon points out, he and his companions had worked hard all night and had not caught anything. These were experienced and successful corporate fishermen. They knew what they were doing and it didn't look terribly promising. Just to add to the challenge, deep-water fishing was normally a night time activity as that is where the fish go at night not during the day and, furthermore, the nets they had were used for night fishing – trammel nets made of linen which were visible to fish during the day and broke easily if there was too large a catch.

However we interpret the miraculous it is worth noting that what Jesus asked the disciples to do was different. It was counter-intuitive and that led to a sense of surprise and wonder. Sometimes discipleship is about being different. About living and working differently. Sometimes we are called within and outside the church to work counter-intuitively, to do things differently not just the way we have always done things. We need to make space for the surprising and the wonderful.[17]

Earlier I shared the story of how I discovered I could swim. Swimming has become something of a metaphor for discipleship for me. A metaphor that took on new meaning when on a family holiday in Austria.

One day we were blessed with glorious hot weather and visited an open-air swimming pool situated next to a beautiful lake. Being very British I thought the odd bit of swimming in the pool, reading a good book and staring at the scenery would be all that was needed for a great day. Whilst staring at the scenery I noticed how many of the locals were forsaking the confines of the pool and swimming out into the lake. After a while I said to my wife and son, 'I'm thinking of going for a swim in the lake.' They both gave me that disbelieving look that only wives and children can do. Undeterred I tiptoed down to the edge of the lake and in a very British male way began to creep into the lake small step by small step. As the look of incredulity grew wider on my family's faces I took the plunge and swam out, surprised at myself and captivated by the wonder of both the scenery and experience. A little later on, having got over the shock of me doing what they never thought I would do, my wife and son joined me and we had a fabulous time. The moment became a reminder of the value in letting go of the familiar to discover the surprising and wonderful.

Call

To return to Simon's story. He hears Jesus sharing the word of God, he begins to get to know him, experiences something special, and then comes the call. There are striking similarities in Luke's account of the call of Simon and the story of the call of Isaiah which reassures us that places of worship as well as places of work can also be places of encounter, call and commission.

In the year that King Uzziah died, I saw the Lord, high and exalted, seated on a throne; and the train of his robe filled the temple. Above him were seraphim, each with six wings: With two wings they covered their faces, with two they covered their feet, and with two they were flying. And they were calling to one another: 'Holy, holy, holy is the LORD *Almighty; the whole earth is full of his glory.' At the sound of their voices the doorposts and thresholds shook and the temple was filled with smoke. 'Woe to me!' I cried. 'I am ruined! For I am a man of unclean lips, and I live among a people of unclean lips, and my eyes have seen the King, the* LORD *Almighty.' Then one of the seraphim flew to me with a live coal in his hand, which he had taken with tongs from the altar. With it he touched my mouth and said, 'See, this has touched your lips; your guilt is taken away and your sin atoned for.' Then I heard the voice of the Lord saying, 'Whom shall I send? And who will go for us?' And I said, 'Here am I. Send me!'*[18]

Biblical commentator Joel Green[19] identifies four key matching episodes in the call stories of Isaiah and Simon.

1. Epiphany or revelation. For Simon this comes through the miraculous catch of fish (Luke 5:4–7), for Isaiah through a heavenly vision (Isaiah 6:1–4). With both there was some sense of God at work for them before the specific moment indentified as their call.

2. Awareness of sin in the presence of holiness. Simon says, 'Go away from me, Lord, for I am a sinful man' (v.8) whilst Isaiah cries, 'Woe to me for I am a man of unclean lips' (v.5).

3. Moment of reassurance. In Luke we have the familiar phrase of Jesus 'Don't be afraid' (v.10b) whilst in Isaiah the seraphim reassures the soon-to-be prophet that his guilt has been taken away and his sin atoned for (v.7).

4. Commissioning. For Simon this comes in the form of a commission to fish for people (v.10b) whilst for Isaiah it comes through his willing response to the apostolic question, 'Who will go for us?' (v.8).

We thought earlier about the revelation that Simon experienced so let's reflect a bit more on the place of holiness, assurance and commission.

Holiness

Simon's first reaction to the holiness of God as experienced through Jesus is to say 'go away from me Lord'. Simon is not unique in saying this to Jesus. Discipleship involves being honest about who we are and our position in relation to God. As Paul reminds us 'all have sinned and fall short of the glory of God'.[20]

In his writings Luke uses the term 'sinner' in what we might call a kindly way. It can denote people who have the honesty to recognise themselves in need of divine redemption and the desire to be better than they are. It can also identify those who are ostracised by others and so stand in the greatest need of gracious invitation and the sort of warm, welcoming community we will consider later when we look at Acts 2. Commenting on Luke 5:10 Howard Marshall says, 'Jesus will not in fact depart from the sinner but calls him into the close association of discipleship.'[21]

Simon moves from a place of fear to a place of fellowship. In the space of three short verses Simon goes from calling Jesus *epistates* or master, a common term for rabbis, to calling him *kyrios* or Lord, a clear recognition that in Jesus he sees the agency of God. As we go on the adventure of discipleship in close association with Jesus then the holiness of the one we follow begins to rub off on our lives in ways that make us more like Him.

Assurance

In his discipleship Simon often needed assurance or reassurance. Tom Wright commenting on his call says, 'If he could have seen a movie of what would happen to him in the next year or two, he might have repeated his plea that Jesus leave him in peace.'[22]

Even the most adventurous of disciples need assurance on a regular basis. It's part of honest discipleship. In the adventure of discipleship we don't know what lies ahead but we do know who is journeying with us. I love the fact that the phrase 'Don't be afraid' occurs 366 times in the Bible. It's a phrase Luke is fond off. It's at the heart of his story of the call of Mary for example, who like Simon encounters God, in her case in the form of the angel or messenger, then reacts with fright, is reassured with the highly personal words 'Do not be afraid, Mary'[23] and is then commissioned to be the one through whom God's son would be born.

Simon Guillebuad is committed to radical adventurous discipleship. His following of Jesus led him from a marketing job in London to hair-raising and sometimes downright dangerous missionary adventures in Burundi, DR Congo, Rwanda and Sudan. Noting that 'worry is the interest we pay on tomorrow's trouble'[24] he, with the sincerity born of experience, confidently asserts that 'God's call will never take us where His grace won't keep us'.[25]

Commission

The call to discipleship is not a call to a private/insular bless me relationship. The call to discipleship is a call to commitment, to a life lived in public, to mission, service and evangelism. Joel Green suggests that for Luke, Simon is representative of all who positively respond to Jesus and become his disciples. He also argues that the call story we have been looking at 'establishes a narrative need for Jesus' followers to participate actively in his ministry'.[26] A Kingdom ministry that Luke presents Jesus announcing by, interestingly, quoting from the prophet Isaiah:

'The Spirit of the Lord is on me, because he has anointed me to proclaim good news to the poor. He has sent me to proclaim freedom for the prisoners and recovery of sight for the blind, to set the oppressed free, to proclaim the year of the Lord's favour.'[27]

The ministry to which we are called may involve going to deep waters. It may involve leaving everything to follow or striving for the radical, world-transforming Kingdom right where we are. And that may involve us getting our finger nails dirty, literally or metaphorically, as we sit with, eat with and support those who are poor; as we come alongside those imprisoned behind bars or deep-seated guilt or grief; as we welcome the refugee and the stranger.

Cost

Like Mark, Luke often stresses the cost of discipleship.[28] For all genuine followers of Jesus discipleship will be costly in one way or another but, again, just a word of caution about the leaving everything to follow phrase in Luke 5:11. Simon and his companions may have left everything that day but they did not leave their assets behind permanently. They had partners in their fishing business who in all probability kept the business going when Simon and co. were travelling with Jesus and may have used the business to support the ministry of Jesus and the twelve. As the resurrection stories remind us, after Jesus was crucified Simon Peter went back to his boats. So, just as Paul was supported in his ministry through his own tent making as well as through the generous gifts of others, Peter was probably supported in his ministry though his own business as well as the hospitality and generosity of others.

The Call to Adventure in John

John's account of the calling of the first disciples is very different to the accounts of Mark, Matthew and Luke. However, whilst the location is different and some different characters are involved, many of the themes we have been exploring are present.

John presents the first disciples of Jesus as 'representatives of belief'.[29] As such there is much we can learn from the disciples as presented in the fourth Gospel. John also widens the use of the term *mathetes* during the course of his Gospel, extending the concept of discipleship from a physical following of Jesus and sharing in his mission to a more 'explicitly spiritual connotation [which] facilitates the transition from the disciples of the historical Jesus to later believers'.[30]

The next day John again was standing with two of his disciples, and as he watched Jesus walk by, he exclaimed, 'Look, here is the Lamb of God!' The two disciples heard him say this, and they followed Jesus. When Jesus turned and saw them following, he said to them, 'What are you looking for?' They said to him, 'Rabbi' (which translated means Teacher), 'where are you staying?' He said to them, 'Come and see.' They came and saw where he was staying, and they remained with him that day. It was about four o'clock in the afternoon. One of the two who heard John speak and followed him was Andrew, Simon Peter's brother. He first found his brother Simon and said to him, 'We have found the Messiah' (which is translated Anointed). He brought Simon to Jesus, who looked at him and said, 'You are Simon son of John. You are to be called Cephas' (which is translated Peter). The next day Jesus decided to go to Galilee. He found Philip and said to him, 'Follow me.' Now Philip was from Bethsaida, the city of Andrew and Peter. Philip found Nathanael and said to him, 'We have found him about whom Moses in the law and also the prophets wrote, Jesus son of Joseph from Nazareth.' Nathanael said to him, 'Can anything good come out of Nazareth?' Philip said to him, 'Come and see.' When Jesus saw Nathanael coming towards him, he said of him, 'Here is truly an Israelite in whom there is no deceit!' Nathanael asked him, 'Where did you come to know me?' Jesus answered, 'I saw you under the fig tree before Philip called you.' Nathanael replied, 'Rabbi, you are the Son of God! You are the King of Israel!' Jesus answered, 'Do you believe because I told you that I saw you under the fig tree? You will see greater things than these.' And he said to him, 'Very truly, I tell you, you will see heaven opened and the angels of God ascending and descending upon the Son of Man.' [31]

John locates the calling of Jesus' first disciples in the context of them being with John the Baptist. Matthew, Mark and Luke don't make this link in their Gospels although intriguingly Luke quotes Peter in Acts saying that Judas' replacement should have 'accompanied us throughout the time that the Lord Jesus went in and out among us, *beginning from the baptism of John*'.[32] We don't have space here to explore all the variants in the Gospel call narratives[33] but the differences do serve as a reminder that the call to follow can and does come in many different ways and that we need to be extremely careful of never becoming too prescriptive as to how anyone begins to follow Jesus. As we thought earlier, and as John makes clear again, when it comes to the adventure of Christian discipleship the initiative is with Jesus. It is up to him how the journey begins.

Witness and Testimony

Whilst the initiative remains with Jesus, John highlights the effect that bearing witness or sharing testimony can have in encouraging others to follow Jesus. John the Baptist points Andrew and his companion to Jesus. Andrew in turn brings his brother Simon to the one he believes to be the Messiah. Philip finds Nathaniel and brings him to Jesus. Andrew and Philip reappear later in the Gospel bringing others to Jesus.[34] As we shall see later when exploring the holy habits of discipleship, healthy disciples help to make and form other disciples. For Andrew and Philip this facet of discipleship was alive and fruitful from the beginning.

Learning and Understanding

The nature of discipleship as adventurous following is explicit in John's call narrative. It is encapsulated in the phrases 'Come and see' and 'Follow me'. The supportive nature of discipleship as learning is more implicit but still strong. Speaking of the Gospel as a whole Raymond Brown argues that 'John presents a conspectus [or summary] of Christian vocation. There is a gradual deepening of insight and a profounder realization of who it is the disciples are following.'[35] In the call narratives this all gets compressed with Andrew moving from addressing Jesus as Rabbi to telling Simon Peter that he has found the Messiah. Meanwhile Nathanael moves from cynicism and scepticism to deep devotional faith.

Whilst our understanding may not deepen so dramatically or quickly, this episode reminds us of the importance of growing in the understanding of, and relationship to, the one we are following. As well as sharing in the activities of his mission. Healthy discipleship is reflective as well as active. In his very helpful book *The Reflective Disciple* Roger Walton explores in depth the importance of reflection, pointing out that: 'Faithful reflection is practised by people who are in an active, living relationship with God. They have begun the journey of faith and are seeking to learn to live better as disciples of Christ, to exercise their faith more effectively in daily living.'[36]

In his subsequent volume *Disciples Together* Roger shares findings of research conducted into what he describes as the formative energies of discipleship. He concludes that for the Christian disciple mission, worship and intentional community are the three primary formative energies. He sees Christian education (or intentional learning) as being supportive of mission, worship and community and happening best in the contexts of these three energies or activities.

For Steven Croft the relationship between action and reflection is also vital in forming disciples. For him Mark 3:14 is a pivotal passage. This is part of Mark's short account of Jesus appointing the twelve disciples as apostles. Bishop Steven notes how Jesus appoints them to 'be with him, and to be sent out'. Here we have a simple but helpful rhythm of discipleship. We gather with Jesus in community with our fellow disciples to reflect and then we go out on the adventure of discipleship and mission. And then we come back to reflect on what we have experienced. Learning supporting the following.

And now back to John.

Grounded in Scripture
In exploring Luke's narrative we noted how the disciples' call came in the context of people listening to Jesus sharing the word of God. In John's story Philip identifies Jesus to Nathanael as the one 'about whom Moses in the law and also the prophets wrote'.[37] So once again at a crucial formative stage the Word of God has an important part to play in forming discipleship.

Encountering the Glorious
John's account of the calling of the first disciples ends with Jesus sharing

a glorious vision with the freshly called Nathanael.

> *'Very truly, I tell you, you will see heaven opened and the angels of God ascending and descending upon the Son of Man.'*[38]

John's Gospel is full of pictures, visions, miracles and signs that reveal the glory of God the Father and God the Son. Immediately after his account of the calling of the first disciples John tells the story of the miracle at the wedding in Cana where Jesus turns water into wine. At the end of the story John says how 'Jesus did this . . . and revealed his *glory*; and his disciples believed in him.'[39] So just as we saw the importance of miracles for Luke here we see the importance of God's glory in Jesus for John and for us in our discipleship and in the encouragement of others pondering or participating in the adventure of discipleship. Glimpses of glory inspire, renew, energise. Wherever and however we are called to live out our discipleship we need such moments to sustain and inspire us and to help us keep on putting one foot after another on the adventure of discipleship. This is true for all disciples including the comparatively few who are 'set apart' by way of ordination.

Whilst writing this book I attended an Ordination Service for Methodist ministers graciously and generously hosted at Liverpool Cathedral by the Anglican Bishop Paul Bayes, and the Dean of the Cathedral, Pete Wilcox. It was a magnificent, uplifting, Spirit-filled time. Those newly ordained spoke of how uplifted, inspired and blessed they were by the glorious occasion. For many of them being ordained was a costly decision – my friend Chris, for example, having left a successful career in accountancy and financial management. It is also a decision that in the words of the ordination service will 'make great demands upon you and upon those close to you.'[40] The glimpses of glory that the ordinands were blessed with in the cathedral that day will be so valuable for the healthy and fruitful development of their discipleship and ministries.

Works in Progress

One of the most reassuring aspects of John's presentations of the disciples is the way in which they are 'not examples of perfect faith, but of positive and typical misunderstandings'.[41] Nathanael's famously grumpy 'Can anything good come out of Nazareth?'[42] is a reminder of the dangers of prejudice and bigotry but also, paradoxically, a point of hope for us all. For if Nathanael could be so wrong and yet be promised that he will 'see heaven opened',[43] what glorious experiences may we who get life and faith mixed up and wrong on a regular basis encounter on the adventure of discipleship? We are works in progress, being changed by grace into the likeness of the one we follow on a journey of transformation that will only be complete in heaven.

Kingdom Adventurers

The call of discipleship is a call to adventure. A call to the new, to the unknown, to the risky, challenging and demanding. But as any adventurer worth their salt knows it is not a call to recklessness or foolishness. We are called to be part of the community of the followers of Jesus. And from the supportiveness of that community we are called to go and live out the life of the Kingdom in the public arena.

For Further Study and Reflection

Personally

Read, compare and reflect upon the call narratives in the four gospels. What do they say to you about the nature of discipleship?

What new challenge may you be being called to at this time?

Locally

In the light of the call narratives reflect on the culture of your local Christian community. Ponder questions such as these (or others that come to mind out of this chapter):

- How adventurous is your church, your fellowship, your small group?
- What sense of the glorious or the holy is there in your gatherings and activities?
- In what ways is your life together grounded in Scripture?

Globally

In anxious and neurotic Western cultures what can we learn from countries that are relatively poor economically but rich spiritually? In particular what can we learn about not being afraid?

And what out of our riches can we share with those in need elsewhere? For example, in compiling the bibliography for this book I have been challenged as to how many books I have on my shelves and can borrow from my local theological college. Might you join me in providing commentaries and other books to churches and pastors in countries where they are scarce?

Biblical Passages to Reflect On

Study one or more of the call passages introduced in this passage with the help of a good commentary or two. The bibliography at the end of this book contains details of commentaries I have found helpful.

Recommended Reading

- Mark Greene, *Fruitfulness on the Frontline.*
- Roger L. Walton, *Disciples Together.*
- Roger L. Walton, *The Reflective Disciple.*

Endnotes

1. Extract from 'Will You Come And Follow Me'/'The Summons' by John L. Bell and Graham Maule. Copyright © 1987 WGRG, c/o Iona Community, Glasgow, G2 3DH, Scotland. Reproduced by permission. www.wildgoose.scot.

2. Mark 1:16–20.

3. Mark 1:18 and Matthew 4:20.

4. Mark 1:16 – 3:12; 3:13 – 6:6; 6:7 – 8:26.

5. Robert A. Guelich, Mark 1 – 8:26, *Word Biblical Commentary 34a*, Dallas: Word Books, 1989, p49.

6. Commenting on John's Gospel Roger Walton points out that 'For John, being close to Jesus is a hallmark of a disciple. Perhaps more than the other Gospel writers, John highlights the time Jesus spends with his disciples.' Roger L. Walton, *Disciples Together*, London: SCM Press, 2014, p28.

7. Donald English, *The Message of Mark*, Leicester IVP, 1992, p53.

8. www.bbc.co.uk/sport/0/football/34261682.

9. Matthew 28:19.

10. Alison Morgan, *The Plural of Disciple is Church*, Wells; Resource, 2015.

11. Some commentators suggesting that he has woven together elements of Mark's succinct call narrative and the post resurrection story known to John of the miraculous catch of fish (John 21:1–14).

12. Luke 5:1–11.

13. Which here is called Gennesaret.

14. Luke 8:2; 7:18–23; Acts 9:32–35; 9:36–42.

15. I. Howard Marshall, *The Gospel of Luke*, Exeter; Paternoster Press, 1978, p199.

16. Luke 4:38–39.

17. If you want to reflect on this further you might want to look at the place of miracles in Luke's writings (see for example Luke 5:17–26; 7:11–16; 13:13; 17:15; 11–18).

18. Isaiah 6:1–8 NIV.

19. Joel Green, *The Gospel of Luke*, Eerdmans, Cambridge, 1997, p233.

20. Romans 3:23.

21. I. Howard Marshall, *The Gospel of Luke*, Exeter; Paternoster Press, 1978, p203.

22. Tom Wright, *Luke for Everyone*, London; SPCK, 2001, p53.

23. Luke 1:30.

24. Simon Guillebaud, *More Than Conquerors*, Oxford: Monarch Books, 2009, p52.

25. Ibid.

26. Joel Green, *The Gospel of Luke*, Eerdmans, Cambridge, 1997, p230.

27. Luke 4:18–19 NIV.

28. Luke 5:11–28; 18:28; 9:57–62; 14:25–33; 19:8.

29. Susan E. Hylen, *Imperfect Believers, Ambiguous Characters in the Gospel of John*, Louisville: John Knox Press, 2009, p59.

30. Andreas J. Köstenberger, *The Mission of Jesus and the Disciples According to the Fourth Gospel*, Grand Rapids: Eerdmans, 1998, p149.

31. John 1:35–51.

32. Acts 1:21–22.

33. Some commentators suggest that John may actually record the first meeting of Jesus with his disciples whilst Matthew, Mark and Luke tell of a subsequent encounter by Lake Galilee.

34. The boy with his loaves and fish (John 6:8) and the Greeks at the Feast (John 12:22).

35. Raymond Brown, *The Gospel According to John (Volume 1)*, London: Geoffrey Chapman, 1966, p77.

36. Roger L. Walton, *The Reflective Disciple*, London: SCM Press, 2012, p115.

37. John 1:45.

38. John 1:51.

39. John 2:11 (emphasis mine).

40. Methodist Worship Book, Trustees for Methodist Church Purposes, 1999, p302.

41. Susan E. Hylen, *Imperfect Believers, Ambiguous Characters in the Gospel of John*, Louisville: John Knox Press, 2009, p60.

42. John 1:46.

43. John 1:51.

3
The Aims of Discipleship

The glory of God is a human being fully alive.
St Irenaeus

A wise person once said that if you aim at nothing you are bound to hit it. We have been reflecting on the nature of discipleship. It is an adventure, a challenge, a transformational journey. We have recognised that a Christian disciple is one who learns as they follow the Jesus who calls them. In looking at the call narratives in the Gospels we have recognised the importance of community, challenge, call, commission, holiness, assurance, witness, learning, scripture and the glorious and miraculous for embarking upon and continuing the adventure of discipleship. But what is the purpose of discipleship? What are we aiming for in making disciples, forming Christian communities and practising holy habits? What outcomes should we expect to see?

In the preface I said that discipleship is about a divinely inspired and divinely infused wholesome humanity that seeks to live generously and graciously in harmony with God and the whole of creation. It is a 24/7 calling and a Kingdom calling to be worked out in every facet of our lives: our relationships and our sense of self; our work and our leisure; our care of creation and struggle for justice. In this chapter I will unpack these statements and in so doing will share thoughts and insights from some noted writers who have contributed much to thinking about the purpose of discipleship.

Kingdom Transformation

In Matthew, Mark and Luke, Jesus begins his ministry before calling the disciples to follow him and he does so by proclaiming the Kingdom. Matthew presents Jesus saying:

> *Repent for the kingdom of heaven has come near.*[1]

Mark has a slightly fuller account of what Jesus said:

> *The time is fulfilled, and the kingdom of God has come near, repent and believe in the good news.*[2]

Meanwhile Luke presents Jesus quoting Isaiah to explain what he is about:

> *The Spirit of the Lord is upon me, because he has anointed me to bring good news to the poor. He has sent me to proclaim release to the captives and recovery of sight to the blind. To let the oppressed go free, to proclaim the year of the Lord's favour.*[3]

before ending the chapter with Jesus saying:

> *I must proclaim the good news of the kingdom of God to the other cities also; for I was sent for this purpose.*[4]

So before Jesus calls anyone to follow him he has declared his purpose, set out his stall, presented his mission statement and revealed what he is about. And in a nutshell it is about the good news of the Kingdom of God. The revelation of the heavenly rule of God on earth. The good news that God loves his creation deeply with a particular passion for the poor, needy and oppressed. The truly radical nature of Jesus' mission statement was in saying that the blessings of heaven could be known on earth and that God's reign (Kingdom) could be experienced as present reality as well as future hope. This is good news for all people as hinted at by the reference to other cities in Luke 4:43.

It is this mission that the first disciples signed up to when they responded to Jesus' call to 'Follow me'. A Kingdom mission of good news and transformation. A mission that disciples of Jesus continue to be called to today. Here we have our first aim or purpose of discipleship. To participate in the Kingdom mission of Jesus; to see God's will and reign on earth as it is in heaven – to quote the 'Disciples Prayer'.[5] To see the world transformed. Transformed into a place where no child is hungry, where no woman is abused. A place where people live in peace. A place of laughter and love, of generosity and grace. A place where God's creation is treated with care and respect and God himself is honoured and worshipped.

Naïve? Crazy? Maybe but so was the idea of walking on the moon or linking all parts of the world by an invisible communication web. And so too was the idea that the son of a carpenter from a backwater provincial town could change the world.

Professor John Hull affirms the all-encompassing, totally transforming vision of the Kingdom that disciples of Jesus individually and collectively are called to pursue. 'The Kingdom of God . . . is the reign of God over all the forces of death, the triumph of love over all the forces of hatred, the triumph of peace over all the forces of violence and warfare.'[6]

Every now and then we have the privilege of experiencing God's Kingdom here on earth in a clear and vivid way. I was blessed with one such experience the day I went to Zac's Place, a fresh expression of church in Swansea.

I encountered a community of self-proclaimed ragamuffins that was one of the most authentic Christian communities I have ever met. In my weaker moments I would gladly smash up or burn many a church notice board that says 'All are welcome' because it is simply not true, unless one totally conforms to the whims and wishes of the controlling powers. At Zac's I met people really trying their very best to make all welcome. The love was tangible. It doesn't matter whether you arrive in a bin bag, a BMW or on a bike. I met many bikers – big guys in leathers and combat trousers who probably could have picked me up in one hand and thrown me through the windows. I met those battered and broken and those with serious addiction issues. Then there are the apparently well-sorted middle-class professionals including the lady with her designer jeans and expensive hairdo who the bikers warmly welcomed as their friend. And the great thing is they are all welcome. There is no inverse snobbery, no resentment of those who have some of the nicer things of life. Just real people trying their best to be real disciples of Jesus.

The 'Zaclicans' highlighted the importance of the value of transformation. Personal transformation (including conversion and discipleship) and the transformation brought about by the struggles for social justice. At Zac's the hungry are fed (the food is great), the naked are clothed, the sick are prayed for and God's word is proclaimed. The Kingdom of God is at hand. The adventure of discipleship is being lived.

Transformed Character

So the big-picture aim of discipleship is the transformation of the world. For the Kingdom of heaven to be real on earth. But the world is made of individuals and a clear focus of teaching in the New Testament is that discipleship is about the transformation of individuals into the likeness or character of Jesus.

For Graham Cray 'Character formation is the object of disciple making'[7] whilst Roger Walton suggests that 'the path of discipleship is a journey of transformation'.[8] In the New Testament this is implied in the

Gospels and we observe the disciples beginning to be formed in Christ-like character as they follow Jesus. Reassuringly for those of us who follow in their footsteps their journeying towards Christ-like character is full of ups and downs, triumphs and failures. They seem to get as much wrong as they get right but critically, poignantly and wonderfully even when they get it most wrong and deny and abandon Jesus, Jesus does not deny and abandon them. Rather he calls them back to the adventure that they began together, entrusts his mission to them and promises the gift of the Spirit to guide and empower them.[9]

The development of Christ-like character as a focus or aim of discipleship becomes more explicit in the epistles. Becoming ever more like Jesus is a constant call[10] and an ultimate aim.[11]

Holy Humanity

Discipleship as we have seen is relational and personal. It flows from the relationship we have with the one who calls us to follow. It is about being in Christ, but when we talk about being 'in Christ' or 'Life in the Spirit' there is a risk that we associate this with a separated lifestyle lived in some hermetically sealed spiritual bubble which keeps us pure and uncontaminated by 'the world'. This risk is accentuated by the way in which the words 'holy' or 'holiness' can be used – words which can be problematic in both every day and specifically Christian usage.

In the book *Holiness and Mission* Professor Morna Hooker points out that 'to be holy originally meant, simply, to be separated, set apart'[12] and that taking this too literally risks creating individuals and communities that are separatist, turned in upon themselves and excluding of others. The kind of 'holy huddles' that are rightly criticised.

Professor Hooker goes on to explain that 'holiness means living according to the revealed character of God'[13] and that the 'true nature of God has been revealed in one who is *truly human*'.[14]

Artists portray Jesus with a halo, to emphasise his otherness, his holiness, and in the process make him less than human. But the incarnation reminds us that God's holiness is about who he is, and about what he reveals himself to be in the person of Jesus. He is not a God who stands apart, but a God who identifies with humanity, a God who gets involved with his creation.[15]

She further suggests that the ancient command 'to be holy as I am holy'[16] is 'a command to be like Christ'.[17] To be holy in a down-to-earth way. The holiness of Jesus touched those with contagious diseases and those who were bleeding. It bestowed dignity upon those who felt like dirt. It feasted and fasted, played with children and prayed. It laughed, cried and bled. It got angry, frustrated and hurt. It was at the centre of celebrations and parties. And it was touched and blessed by the kindness of friends and strangers alike.

Judy Hirst tells of a morning she had set apart to prepare for a meeting with an editor who might have been interested in publishing the book that became *Struggling to be Holy*.

I had set aside the morning to think but the door bell had rung and a very distressed young woman was there to see me. She had been abused as a child and, whilst usually coping well, occasionally found herself in a very painful place. There is never much that can be said at such times. All that really helps is to be with her and to hold her as she cries. So that was how the morning passed and no thinking was done. Lunchtime found me dashing to the meeting with a sinking feeling in my heart. How had I got myself into this embarrassing position? In exasperation, I said out loud to myself, 'I don't know anything about holiness!' and it was as if a voice asked, 'So what have you just been doing?' I was blank for a moment until I remembered the morning of sitting with someone in pain. 'Isn't that something about holiness then?' the voice replied.[18]

True holiness is heavenly and human. It is holistic. Divine and down to earth. It makes the ordinary, special. In his magnificent book *Running Over Rocks*, Ian Adams presents a picture of spirituality and discipleship that embraces the 'normal' and the 'sacred', that aspires 'to be goodness and to bring goodness'[19] by living in harmony with ourselves (body, mind and spirit), other people, creation and the 'love that holds everything together', namely God; the Father who created us, the Son who saves and calls us, and the Spirit who inspires and fills us. True holiness is not just personal. It is social, relational and communal. It is evidenced in equality, justice and peace.

Holy Struggle

As we will see in Chapter 4 the pathway of Christian discipleship is one that inevitably involves struggle, sacrifice and suffering for true discipleship is cruciform, cross shaped. But as faithful disciples down the ages have found, it is also a pathway of wonder, joy and true pleasure.

In the film *Chariots of Fire* the Christian athlete Eric Liddell says, 'I believe God made me for a purpose, but he also made me fast. And when I run I feel his pleasure.' Liddell was diligent in practising the holy habits of discipleship. He was willing to make all sorts of sacrifices – losing the chance of a gold medal by not running on a Sunday – but he also enjoyed, took pleasure in, being the person God had made him to be.

He went on to serve as a missionary in China, being imprisoned by the Japanese when they invaded China during the Second World War. He became a leader and organiser at the camp, but food, medicine and other supplies were scarce. While fellow missionaries formed sanctimonious cliques and acted selfishly, Liddell busied himself by helping the elderly, teaching at the camp school Bible classes, arranging games and by teaching science to the children, who referred to him as Uncle Eric.

Liddell knew how to play as well as how to pray. Such discipleship is holy, winsome and deeply attractive. It models a way of life that honours, brings fulfilment and pleasure, and inspires others to explore the adventure of following Jesus.

Whole Life Disciples

Someone once said that Jesus did not come to make us more religious but came to make us fully human. As our consideration of holiness has hinted, the adventure of discipleship is to be lived out in the whole of our lives. Martyn Atkins puts it this way:

> Discipleship of Jesus Christ shapes the whole of life, not just the 'religious bits'. It's about us as individuals and human beings, and involves us totally, body, mind and spirit. It's also, equally, about our interconnectedness with others, in groups, congregations, families, through our work and leisure, in communities local and global.[20]

As we noted in the previous chapter when exploring Mark's call account, for most Christian disciples, most of the time, the adventure of discipleship is lived out in the places where we are set. Our homes, places of work, leisure and service. It is there we struggle to be holy, it is there we bear witness, it is there we make a difference. For a small proportion of our time we gather with our fellow disciples for worship, fellowship and service together.

Mark Greene, Tracy Cotterell and their colleagues at the London Institute for Contemporary Christianity (LICC) have been amongst the most prominent people advocating a whole life approach to discipleship. On the LICC website they say this: 'We may engage in specific mission and service together, but this will never be at the expense of realising that our primary calling is to make a difference where we find ourselves most of the time.'[21]

So when it comes to the holy habits that we will explore in Part 2 of this book it is vital that when we meet together to practise the habits we do so in a way that resources the whole life discipleship we are called to. We also need to find ways to practise the habits when we are scattered, following Jesus in our homes, places of work and communities.

Over the years Shona has introduced hundreds of children to Jesus. She has taught them to pray, shared biblical stories with them, introduced them to Christian worship and engaged them in Kingdom activities including the support of Fairtrade and providing gifts for other children by filling shoeboxes with toys. All at the same time as equipping the children with the foundational learning skills that they need to flourish, and being a listening, prayerful support to colleagues struggling with illness and bereavement.

Shona is not ordained or employed by the church. She is a primary school teacher faithfully doing her best to follow Jesus and bring transformation to the lives of the children she serves and the community in which the school is set. All at the same time as equipping the children with the learning skills necessary for life.

Full Life Disciples

In John's Gospel in particular the way of Jesus is presented in terms of a vibrant, full life. A life of the creative, life-giving energy of God. It is a dynamic, colourful, inspiring, energising image. In the prologue to the fourth Gospel, John celebrates that in Jesus, God's Word made flesh, was '*life*, and the life was the light of all people'.[22] C.K. Barrett points out in his colossus of a commentary that 'Life and light are essential elements in the Old Testament *creation* narrative. God gives life'.[23] He goes on to note how 'The life was the essential *energy* of the Word'[24]. God forgive us if we ever suggest in our churches and personal witness that discipleship is coloured in fifty shades of dull.

As we read on in John and see that life and light in action we encounter Jesus saying, 'I came that they may have life, and have it *abundantly*.'[25] There is a richness here way beyond anything money can buy.

When I visited Barbados I went for a walk one day. The walk took me out into the countryside far away from the cruise ships, tourist hotels and designer boutiques. As I walked I heard a woman singing joyfully, beautifully. As I drew nearer I saw the lady sweeping the immaculate step of her small tin-roofed bungalow, as her chickens ran round the little garden in which her vegetables grew. The songs she sang were hymns and the smile on her face was one of beatific, heavenly joy. She was the personification of life in all its fullness.

God-given abundant life is not confined to the Caribbean. It can be found in Stoke-on-Trent too. Neil Baldwin is a disciple of Jesus. For a while he was a lay preacher but his whole life is an outworking of biblical teaching. The BAFTA award-winning BBC film *Marvellous* tells the inspiring story of his life:

> Speaking about the release of the film he said, 'My friends who came along to the premiere said, "You've put God in it first" – and that's how it should be. If you've got no Lord, you are lost. God is always working in me, and through all the people that I've met.'[26]

Neil has always had a great appetite for life. He struggled at school with various learning difficulties but has achieved a great deal. He worked in a butcher's for many years before joining a circus to play the part of 'Nello the Clown'. When the circus moved on without him he went to Keele University, where his mother had a cleaning job. He appointed himself to the role of (unofficial) greeter to new students – a role that was so appreciated it was rewarded by an honorary degree. He also got to manage the university's unofficial football team which is named after him. His career reached its zenith when he talked his way into becoming the kit man and mascot of his beloved football team Stoke City. This man of humble origins became a holy presence in the very earthy world of the football changing room. And it was that down-to-earth holiness that inspired the film makers to produce *Marvellous*.

A Heavenly Destination
Discipleship is both a down-to-earth and a heavenly calling. In one of the most poignant verses in the Bible Jesus, in the midst of his own agony on the cross, says to the broken man who knows his need of forgiveness, 'Truly I tell you, today you will be with me in Paradise.'[27]

Bruce Milne in his book *Know the Truth* said, 'To see and know

God is the essence of the heavenly life, the fount and source of all bliss. As Psalm 16:11 says, "You will fill me with joy in your presence, with eternal pleasure at your right hand."[28] So Milne goes on to say, 'We may be confident that the crowning wonder of our experience will be in the heavenly realm with endless exploration of that unutterable beauty, majesty, love, holiness, power, joy and grace which is God himself.'[29] That is the ultimate destination of the adventure of discipleship.

Perhaps the most moving moment in my ministry came when I made my last visit to Tom, a dear retired miner in Durham. I had visited Tom many times to talk and pray as he, with dignity and courage, lived with the cancer that was killing him. The final time I visited, Tom had virtually disappeared. His once strong body now little more than a skeleton. We knew Tom didn't have long left in this world, but we also both believed deeply that the fullness of heaven was waiting. As we prayed that day and anticipated Tom seeing Jesus face to face, Tom took my hands and kissed them. And in that moment heaven and earth met.

When the New Testament was being written the prevalent view was that heaven is essentially the dwelling place of God. So when John says, 'the Word became flesh and made his dwelling among us,'[30] he was saying in Jesus, heaven came down to earth. The truly radical message that Jesus preached, taught and demonstrated through his miracles, especially his healings and exorcisms, was that the Kingdom of heaven was to be seen, experienced and enjoyed right here, right now on earth as it is in heaven.[31]

As we noted above when thinking about Kingdom Transformation, part of our calling as disciples today is to discern, point to, and pray and work for more signs of heaven on earth. Not just to prepare ourselves and others for the moment when we die but to experience, enjoy and expand heaven on earth now. Heaven we see in the smiling eyes of the hungry child being fed and in the face of the young woman who has had a tough life being baptised as a sign of her being born again. Heaven we see wherever God's will is done, God's blessing is known, and God's just and gracious reign is acknowledged and lived.

Communities of Transformation

Whilst recognising that the primary context for the seeking of Kingdom transformation and the exercising of discipleship for most of us will be in the various contexts that we spend most of our lives, it is vital to not lose sight of the fact that right from the very start Jesus called and gathered people into community. Community with him and with each other. Community that will model heaven on earth. Community that will pray for Kingdom transformation. Community that will support personal transformation, the struggle for holiness and the day-to-day adventures of discipleship lived out at work, home and in the communities. And community that will grow.

It might be stating the obvious but right from the beginning there was a dynamic of growth in the discipleship community of Jesus. The two became twelve. Women joined the men. Seventy were sent out in mission. Alongside the numerical growth there was also growth in understanding, relationship and Kingdom impact. As we will see when we come to explore the holy habit of making more disciples, the dynamic of growth continued after the outpouring of the Spirit at Pentecost. Again it may be stating the obvious but the more growth there is in the number and depth of disciples and the number of discipleship communities, the more Kingdom transformation there will be.

David Watson in his seminal book *Discipleship* argues that 'the goal of evangelism is the formation of Christian community'.[32] Not as an end in itself but so that 'God's plan for the healing of creation'[33] can be fulfilled. Here we come full circle with disciples being transformed as they follow Jesus, supported by Christian communities, living out their discipleship in their day-to-day lives with the ultimate aim of seeing creation healed as God's Kingdom comes on earth as it is in heaven.

We will return to the vital role of community when we consider holy habitats at the start of Part 2.

Aiming High

So what are we aiming for when we practise the holy habits of discipleship? We are looking to nurture adventurous followers of Jesus who, as they share in his mission and live out their discipleship in their day-to-day lives, are being transformed into his holy, down-to-earth likeness. People who live full, attractive, colourful, creative lives. All supported by transformational communities full of life and grace, exemplars of the heavenly Kingdom that is both an experience to be realised now and the final destination of the adventure.

Suggestions for Further Reflection and Action

Personally
What are you aiming for?

What does holiness mean to you?

How do you live holiness practically on a day to day basis?

In what ways is your life a sign of the Kingdom? How might it be a little more so tomorrow?

How 'whole life' is your discipleship?

Locally
In what ways is your Christian community a sign of the Kingdom? How might it be visibly so in the wider community?

In what ways is your Christian community growing? How might you be more intentional about the various aspects of growth explored in this chapter?

Globally
What can you learn from the dynamic growth of Christian communities in other parts of the world?

How might your fellowship partner with a growing fellowship in another country both to support them or to learn from them?

A Biblical Passage to Reflect On
- John 21:15–19

What do you notice in this passage?

What will you do or change in the light of what you have read and noticed?

Recommended Reading
- Ian Adams, *Running Over Rocks.*
- David Watson, *Discipleship.*
- Robert J. Wicks, *Touching the Holy.*

Endnotes

1. Matthew 3:2.

2. Mark 1:15.

3. Luke 4:18–19.

4. Luke 4:43.

5. Michael Green suggests that the prayer we often call the Lord's Prayer should be called the Disciples' Prayer and that we should call what is often known as the High Priestly Prayer of Jesus in John the Lord's Prayer instead.

6. John M. Hull, *Mission Shaped Church, A Theological Response*, London: SCM, 2006.

7. freshexpressions.org.uk/news/grahamcray/reader-nov11.

8. Roger L. Walton, *Disciples Together*, London: SCM Press, 2014, p8.

9. For more on this you may wish to read the concluding chapters of the Gospels. In particular the restoration of Peter in John 21:15–19 and the Great Commission in Matthew 28:16–20.

10. Galatians 2:20.

11. 2 Corinthians 3:18, Ephesians 4:13 and 1 John 3:3.

12. Morna D. Hooker, and Francis Young, *Holiness and Mission*, London: SCM, 2010, p4.

13. Ibid, p5.

14. Ibid, p9 emphasis mine.

15. Ibid, p9.

16. Leviticus 20:26 and quoted at 1 Peter 1:16.

17. Morna D. Hooker, and Francis Young, *Holiness and Mission*, London: SCM, 2010, p12.

18. Judy Hirst, *Struggling to be Holy*, London: Darton, Longman and Todd, 2008, p13.

19. Ian Adams, *Running Over Rocks*, Norwich: Canterbury Press, 2013, pxv.

20. Martyn Atkins, *Discipleship and the People Called Methodists*, Peterborough: Trustees for Methodist Church Purposes, 2010, p55.

21. licc.org.uk/imagine-church/the-big-picture

22. John 1:4 (emphasis mine).

23. C.K. Barrett, *The Gospel According to St John, Second Edition*, London: SPCK, 1978, p157 (emphasis mine).

24. Ibid, p158 (emphasis mine).

25. John 10:10 (emphasis mine).

26. lichfield.anglican.org/ournews/marvellous/.

27. Luke 23:43.

28. Bruce Milne, *Know the Truth*, Leicester: IVP, 1982, p278.

29. Ibid.

30. John 1:14 NIV.

31. For more on heaven I would recommend Paula Gooder's book Heaven. See bibliography for details.

32. David Watson, *Discipleship*, London: Hodder and Stoughton, 1981, p41.

33. Ibid.

4

Suffering and the Sacrificial Nature of Discipleship

'When Christ calls a man, he bids him come and die'[1]

These are the startling words with which David Watson began the first chapter of his seminal book *Discipleship*. He attributes them to Dietrich Bonhoeffer, the young German Lutheran pastor who publicly denounced and defied the Nazis, was imprisoned by them and then executed for allegedly taking part in a plot to kill Adolf Hitler. He was killed just two weeks before the Allies liberated the prison in which he was being held. On his personal adventure of discipleship Bonhoeffer was willing to sacrifice himself for the values of the Kingdom and the peace and well-being of others. In the darkness of the Nazi shadow the cost of being a follower of Jesus could be all too clear. As too of course, many million times, could the cost of being a Jew like Jesus. Writing from prison to his best friend Eberhard Bethge, Bonhoeffer said:

Please don't ever get anxious or worried about me, but don't forget to pray for me – I'm sure you don't. I am so sure of God's guiding hand that I hope I shall always be kept in that certainty. You must never doubt that I'm travelling with gratitude and cheerfulness along the road where I'm being led. My past is brim-full of God's goodness, and my sins are covered by the forgiveness of Christ crucified. I'm most thankful for the people I have come close to, and I only hope that they never have to grieve about me, but that they, too, will always be certain of, and thankful for, God's mercy and forgiveness.[2]

As I write this book on the habits of discipleship I am struck by how much Bonhoeffer was appreciative of and dependent upon these practices – prayer and fellowship in particular – when his sacrificial following of Jesus has taken him to a place of darkness and danger. I am also struck by his thankfulness.

Mercifully not all who follow Jesus are called to physically die for him. However, as we noted in Chapter 1, there are still those who are literally laying down their lives in faithfulness to the Jesus they follow, most notably in Iraq and Syria. Much of this is happening in some of the most ancient centres of Christianity. Many are suffering horrific and savage brutality and pain. Some are literally taking up their cross as they are crucified. At the same time Jewish communities are being attacked, with many Jews heading 'home' to Israel and being housed on disputed land, only adding to tensions and grievances.

It is beyond my competence to even begin to suggest either how any of these problems could be resolved or how the life of a Christian disciple should be lived in such circumstances. But I have started this chapter with stories of extreme suffering for two reasons.

Firstly so that we can be mindful of others living out their discipleship in very different circumstances. In the suggestions for further reflection or action at the end of each chapter I have included a number of thoughts for reflection or action that seek to connect with those who pay the highest price in terms of the costs of following Jesus.

Secondly I pause to reflect on others in the hope that it might put some of the costs we pay into perspective. Because I am a follower of Jesus I have been the recipient of some insults, some abuse (sadly as much within the Christian community as without), may have missed out on the odd job or promotion and have certainly earned a lot less than I could. But when I see or hear about what others suffer for their association with Jesus these are all put into perspective and remind me of what I signed up for. A life of adventure, yes. A life in all its fullness, definitely. But also a life of challenge, struggle and sacrifice. Jesus and the heroes and heroines of the faith are totally honest with us. Their teaching and their stories tell us very clearly that the way of discipleship is costly. Which is why it's so important that we are sustained by healthy communities and the ancient and yet ever new habits of discipleship that we will explore shortly.

Always Surprised by Joy

It is humbling and inspiring to be with those whose faithful following of Jesus through grievous suffering has transformed them into a saintliness that we behold with awe. A striking characteristic of such people is their thankfulness and joy. Bonhoeffer is a well-known and inspirational figure. Less well known, but just as inspirational, is a lady called Joy from Stourbridge.

Joy was orphaned as a young child. After basic schooling she began work in a laundry before going on to various cleaning jobs. She never married and lived in a small council bungalow with her cat. In worldly terms she achieved very little. In Kingdom terms she achieved more than most of us.

Like St Paul many years before she learnt the art of contentment.[3] One day I visited her in her home and found her with two friends contentedly listening to the radio and enjoying a big pot of tea. If I had given them a million pounds they could not have been happier.

Joy was faithful in prayer, reading the Bible (gratefully accepting help as her reading was not strong), worship and fellowship and, like the widow commended by Jesus,[4] she gave generously of her time and financial resources. Her purse was always open when there was a charitable event or a disaster appeal. And her cleaning skills kept the chapel spotless.

Joy taught me so much. I had never been very comfortable with the Good News Bible's use of the word happy rather than blessed in the beatitudes of Jesus. Until the day Joy showed me the happiness of being blessed even when suffering. As she lay in her hospice bed she looked at me and said, 'Andrew, I'm so happy.' Almost invisible due to cancer but translucent with joy this saintly lady was so happy to have enjoyed her life, she was happy for the care and love of friends old and new, and so happy at the prospect of being with Jesus. The happiest person I have ever met.

Human Condition

The adventure of discipleship will involve sacrifice and suffering firstly and simply because we are human and suffering is part of the mystery of the human condition from which disciples of Jesus are not exempt. I am writing this part of the book in the immediate aftermath of an horrendous earthquake in Nepal which, at the time of writing, has claimed 6000 lives and left a nation destitute and despairing. Every life lost is a tragedy and amongst those who died were many Christians. *Christianity Today's* website shared this story:

Tamang clapped and sang along as the remnants of her husband's Kathmandu church gathered for a noon prayer one week after a massive earthquake collapsed the 'roof of the world.' Tamang lost her husband Maila, her sister, and three other family members when Vision of Salvation Church, which rented rooms in a four-storey commercial building in the Swayambu area of Nepal's capital, collapsed with 62 worshippers present. Seventeen members of the Pentecostal church, where Tamang's husband served as an elder, died, including senior pastor Elia Ghale and his son.

'We cannot decide our future or what happens to us,' she said, surrounded by cracked walls. 'Even after the world, we will be with God.'[5]

A full exploration of the problem of suffering is beyond the scope of this book but the consistent testimony of disciples of Jesus over the centuries is that God's presence with them in the places of deepest darkness and suffering has provided the strength and sustenance to keep living, keep believing, and keep going.

> My dear friend Jeff Reynolds was an extraordinary man. The son of a boxer, he never even entered a church or thought of Jesus until he was in his twenties. To his astonishment, having embarked on the adventure of discipleship he ended up getting ordained. Alongside his regular ministerial duties this down to earth holy bloke was chaplain to a football club and a prison where he learned helpful skills like how to break into your car when you lock the keys inside. He captained an Anglican Diocesan cricket team which, as a Methodist, gave him particular pleasure, allowing him to order two bishops around (moving them diagonally, of course). And he played in a band, The Smiling Strangers, for whom he wrote many songs.
>
> One of his finest is called 'Covenant'[6] and is based on the Covenant prayer of discipleship written by John Wesley. In the song and in the Spirit of the Covenant prayer Jeff explains how he is willing to be put to suffering even to shame, 'as long as you're there with me'.[7] Jeff lived his discipleship in the light of that relationship. It sustained him in all he was and did, and in his dying at the cruelly early age of fifty-three.

If you would like to explore more fully the mystery of discipleship and suffering, and the testimony to the power and peace of God's presence in the most trying of circumstances, there are many helpful resources available. I would particularly commend the books of Sheila Cassidy.[8] Sheila was arrested and tortured when serving as a missionary in Chile and went on to be the medical director of a hospice. She concludes her book *Sharing the Darkness* by saying:

> Right at the heart of the mystery of suffering is the grace that sustains us all, carers and cared for alike. It comes as freely and as surely as the

sunrise, piercing the blackness of grief and despair, restoring once again the hope of things unseen.[9]

Part of the Call

Living sacrificially is integral to the adventure of following Jesus. When we considered the callings of the first disciples we noted how this was so, right from the outset as 'they left everything and followed him'.[10] Whilst this leaving did not involve a complete severing of ties or selling of everything it was none the less costly in terms of personal ambition, relationships and earning potential. And costly, too, for their families and friends. We don't bear the cost of discipleship alone.

In the Gospels there are many symbols which represent the sacrificial nature of Christian discipleship. The cross is of course the supreme symbol and we also have the narrow way[11] and the yoke.[12] Reflecting on the image of the yoke we find these words in the 1975 version of the Methodist Covenant Service preceding the prayer of discipleship commitment:

> Beloved in Christ, let us again claim for ourselves this Covenant which God has made with his people, and take the yoke of Christ upon us.
>
> To take this yoke upon us means that we are content that he appoint us our place and work, and that he himself be our reward.
>
> Christ has many services to be done: some are easy, others are difficult; some bring honour, others bring reproach; some are suitable to our natural inclinations and material interests, others are contrary to both. In some we may please Christ and please ourselves, in others we cannot please Christ except by denying ourselves. Yet the power to do all things is given us in Christ, who strengthens us.[13]

John and Mary Bramley are a lovely Christian couple from my home town of Stafford. John lived out his discipleship as an orthopaedic surgeon whilst Mary lived hers as a nurse. In addition John was a lay preacher and together they hosted a fellowship group in their home.

Having given of themselves gladly and generously, when the time came for retirement no-one could have begrudged them a retirement filled with grandchildren, cruises, coach trips and tea cakes at garden centres. But these extraordinary, ordinary disciples were willing to sacrifice that for a few years and went to serve as medical missionaries in a leprosy mission hospital in Bhutan. It was deeply humbling to hear John explaining why they were going, saying that they could not pray the prayers they prayed and sing the hymns and songs they sang without being willing to respond to the call of Jesus. And so they went to share in the healing, loving work of Jesus in that far away country. Writing at the age of eighty-one, having been back home for sixteen years, survived a heart attack and now surrounded by grandchildren, John said:

> It has been my Christian faith and experience that in spite of adverse circumstances, sometimes created by my own failures, and sometimes beyond my control, that ultimately all things have worked together for good in my life, with undeserved blessings and strong hope for the future.[14]

Suffering by Association

Living sacrificially in obedience to the call of Jesus may also involve suffering because of our association with the one we follow. This could be in the form of snide comments and insults. We may find ourselves excluded from conversations or opportunities because of our beliefs and values. And occasionally the suffering may be even more painful. This was literally so for Sean Stillman.

> Sean is a Harley-riding, leather-wearing biker. He is also the minister at Zac's Place, the fresh expression of church that we visited in Chapter 3. He is one of the most Christ-like people I have ever met. He looks the part for starters – Google him and you will see what I mean. He builds Kingdom community, teaches God's word, feeds the hungry, clothes the naked, heals the hurting and befriends the stranger. He also literally turned the other cheek and got a beating

when at a motorcycle festival other bikers wanted to punish someone for the crimes of paedophile priests that had been high profile in the news. The entirely innocent Sean, wearing a cross on the back of his leathers, took the beating without striking back, suffering for his association with Jesus that others had so discredited by their crimes.

Part of the Transformative Journey of Holiness

Living sacrificially is at the heart of the adventure of discipleship. When Jesus calls us, he calls us to die to self and live for him. So easy to write but so hard to do. In the last chapter we noticed how one of the aims of discipleship, that John's Gospel in particular presents, is to experience life in all its fullness. Matthew, Mark and Luke share a piece of teaching by Jesus that explains how the way to life is the sacrificial way of denying self.

> 'If any want to become my followers, let them deny themselves and take up their cross and follow me. For those who want to save their life will lose it, and those who lose their life for my sake will find it. For what will it profit them if they gain the whole world but forfeit their life? Or what will they give in return for their life?[15]

For Paul this is all about dying to sin and being raised with Christ, a theme he explores in Romans 6. A full exposition of the nature of sin is beyond the scope of this book but one definition that I have found enormously helpful over the years is that sin is a small word with a big I in the middle. A definition that helps us understand that sin is essentially a distorted view of self that puts me at the centre of the universe. Selfishness in short. Selfishness that damages, even denies sometimes, our relationships— our relationships with God, creation and our fellow human beings: going against the life-giving rules of loving God and our neighbour as ourselves.

And here we have the irony of holy living. The pathway of selfish living is so seductive. But ultimately it is so destructive as the teaching of Jesus above makes abundantly clear. And when we embrace the self-giving, loving way of Jesus what do we find? Life in all its fullness.

Footballer Cyrille Regis was living every school boy's dream. Playing centre forward for West Brom and England he had more money, cars and women than any loud-mouthed bore in the pub could boast of. But sadly, like many others in his profession, the glitz and the glamour took its toll and Cyrille began to fall apart with a string of drinking, gambling and relationship issues. Having hit rock bottom Cyrille responded to an invitation from a friend, cricketer Ron Headley, to go to church. There he was led to a personal relationship with Jesus and the adventure of discipleship began. A lot of issues and relationships needed to be sorted and he had to work out how to be a Christian in the often unforgiving culture of the dressing room. Interestingly, in his autobiography Cyrille talks of his prayer of commitment 'as the beginning of his conversion'.[16] The transformational pathway of holiness has been challenging but, symbolised by his baptism, he testifies to how 'a new Cyrille was born'.[17] A content Cyrille at peace with God, his family and himself. A self-giving Cyrille who mentors young men and supports charitable work in Africa. And a Cyrille who is still honoured as a legend at West Brom. I was there recently when he was Guest of Honour for the day, walking around the pitch to the warm acclamation of the crowd.

The Importance of Holy Habits and Habitats

Sacrifice is at the heart of discipleship and suffering, to a greater or lesser extent, is inevitable on the adventure. Which makes the habitats and habits we will go on to explore in Part 2 so vital. Yes, God in his grace does sustain us directly by his Spirit as the Scriptures and saints bear witness, but God has also given us these habits to practise in community, and in our dispersed contexts alike. As we practise them so the fruits of holiness and Christ-like character emerge and blossom, along with the resilience, strength and faith to keep going.

In her deeply honest and inspiring book *Travelling to Infinity*, which inspired the Oscar-winning film *The Theory of Everything*, Jane Hawking lays bare the massive struggles she had caring for Stephen, providing for her family and maintaining her own sense of worth. She also testifies to the way she has been strengthened on her incredible adventure both through providential provision[18] and through the holy habits of prayer, fellowship, biblical teaching, worship and generosity that she practised (sometimes incurring the derision of Stephen) with and through her local church.

A Transformational Adventure

So Jesus calls us, as he called his very first disciples, to the adventure of following him. Whether we are a cleaner with no qualifications or a doctor of modern languages who happens to have been married to the world's most famous physicist. Younger or older, richer or poorer. In vigorous health or crippled by illness. Jesus calls us to share his mission of Kingdom transformation. A calling that is sacrificial and will involve suffering to a greater or lesser extent. A calling that will involve our personal transformation from selfishness to holiness and introduce us to life in all its fullness.

Suggestions for Further Reflection and Action

Personally

If you are in a tough place at the moment take a little time to pray, being honest with God as to what you are thinking and feeling. Pray that as you come to consider the holy habits they may be a renewed means of grace for you and that you will see how these ancient practices can be a source of blessing for you afresh.

If life is good at the moment pray for those who are suffering or struggling. Does the Spirit bring a particular person to mind? If so, what could you do practically this week to help, encourage or support them?

Locally

How might your church partner with or support those who are suffering in your local community? Is there a hospice or refugee centre or victim support group that you could partner with or offer hospitality to?

What space is there in your gatherings for worship or fellowship to bring the needs of those who suffer to God? How balanced are your choices of songs? Are they all praise or worship or are there times of lament too? In what ways might the broken bread of Holy Communion be offered as a prayer for those who suffer and how could it be taken as a gift to them?

Globally

Individually or collectively get involved with an organisation which campaigns on behalf of those who suffer cruelty, persecution or injustice. Open Doors and Amnesty International are two well-known first-class examples but there are many others.

Seek out and befriend those who have fled their own countries as a result of violent suffering and persecution.

A Biblical Passage to Reflect On
- Matthew 16:24–26

What do you notice in this passage?

What will you do or change in the light of what you have read and noticed?

Recommended Reading

- Dietrich Bonhoeffer, *The Cost of Discipleship.*
- Sheila Cassidy, *Good Friday People.*
- Sheila Cassidy, *Sharing the Darkness.*

Endnotes

1. David Watson, *Discipleship*, London: Hodder and Stoughton, 1981, p19.

2. Dietrich Bonhoeffer, *Letters and Papers from Prison*, London: SCM Press, 2001, p148.

3. Philippians 4:11.

4. Mark 12:41–44.

5. http://www.christianitytoday.com/ct/2015/may-web-only/nepal-christians-return-worship-after-earthquake-churches.html.

6. http://www.cdbaby.com/Artist/TheSmilingStrangers.

7. 'Covenant' written by Jeff Reynolds, published by Maori Music.

8. Especially *Good Friday People* and *Sharing the Darkness.*

9. Sheila Cassidy, *Sharing the Darkness*, London: Darton, Longman and Todd, 1988.

10. Luke 5:11.

11. Matthew 7:13–14.

12. Matthew 11:29.

13. *The Methodist Service Book*, The Methodist Conference Office, 1975.

14. John Bramley, *Remember Who You Represent*, Sandy: Authors on Line, 2009.

15. Matthew 16:24–26.

16. Cyrille Regis, *Cyrille Regis My Story*, London: Andre Deutsch, 2010, p191.

17. Ibid, p194.

18. Hawking, Jane, *Travelling to Infinity*, Richmond: Alma Books, 2008, p256.

5

Signs and Wonders

*Awe came upon everyone, because many wonders and signs were being
done by the apostles.*
Acts 2:43

I once met a man who had died and come back to life. A walking sign
and wonder. His name is Fabrice Muamba whom we met as a family
when we were in the audience for the Sky TV show *Soccer AM*. For
those who don't like football he was also on a Christmas edition of
Strictly Come Dancing.

On 17 March 2012 Fabrice was playing for Bolton Wanderers in an
FA Cup match at Tottenham Hotspur. Part way through the first half
he collapsed, his head hitting the ground as he fell. As it bounced he
was still alive. When it bounced again he was dead. His heart stopped
beating for 78 minutes but not only did he survive, he has gone on to
live a full life. A life of gladness and generosity. He begins his book *I'm
Still Standing* with an expression of gratitude:

Thank you. Two small words that make all the difference. And two words that will never do justice to the many people who have made sure I'm still here, alive and well today.

First and foremost I'd like to thank God for giving me health, happiness and family and for also making sure I received the specialist care I needed to save my life.[1]

Fabrice attributes the miracle of his survival to both God and the people who came to his rescue. For him God was operative directly by the Spirit, through the prayers of many, the healing skills of the medics who attended him and the love of those closest to him.

Signs and Wonders in Acts

When we explored the call narratives in Chapter 2 we noted that Dr Luke is not shy when it comes to the place of miracles. His Gospel and Acts are full of them (note the use of the word 'many' in Acts 2:43). In his Gospel, Luke includes more examples of signs and wonders than Matthew, Mark and John do. In Acts the apostles continue the miraculous ministry of Jesus as well as his teaching.

For Luke signs and wonders are significant for a number of reasons. They,

1. Bestow physical benefits on those blessed by them.[2]
2. Authenticate the identity of Jesus 'as the one to come' and the one in whom 'there is salvation'.[3]
3. Provide signs of the immanence of the Kingdom of God.[4]
4. Form part of the Christian witness and produce faith.[5]

James Dunn argues that:

We need not doubt that it is a sound historical fact that many healings of a miraculous sort did occur in the early days of the first Christian communities and of the early Christian mission.[6]

He supports this view by putting the testimonies of Paul[7] and the writer of the letter to the Hebrews[8] alongside the stories recorded by Luke. He also points out that there were others at the time of the early church who were performing what could be described as signs and wonders and is frustrated that Luke often presents 'better' miracles rather than 'distinctive ones'.

Signs and Wonders Today

There are many different views on signs and wonders amongst Christians today. They range from the totally dismissive (arguing that if they ever happened they ceased to happen after the apostolic period described in the New Testament) to the obsessive (which is disappointed if there have not been at least ten miracles before the cornflakes have been put back in the cupboard after breakfast).

Many of the newer and growing Christian communities in the UK and around the world are keen to see signs and wonders in their fellowships and the communities they serve. There is not space to survey the whole panoply of views on signs and wonders here so in the context of this book I offer the following reflection. I think we need a bigger picture of signs and wonders. Whenever and wherever we see people being blessed physically, mentally, spiritually or relationally, justice done and truth prevail, selfishness surrendered and generous sharing, or broken lives made whole, there we see *signs* of God's goodness and *wonders* of his love.

Whenever these signs and wonders are done in the name of Jesus they, like the signs and wonders of Acts, have the potential to:

1. Bestow benefits (physical, mental, spiritual or social) on those blessed by them.
2. Authenticate the identity of Jesus when done in his name.
3. Provide signs of the immanence of the Kingdom of God.
4. Form part of the Christian witness and produce faith.

Some of these signs and wonders may be the result of miraculous persistence. Others may be the consequence of a miraculous moment.

Don't Make God Too Small

This is the heading of a section in David Wilkinson's very helpful book *When I Pray, What Does God Do?* David is a scientist and a theologian with doctorates in both astrophysics and theology. In science in particular he understands things that make my head hurt just by thinking about them but, as with all great communicators, he has the skill to present the complicated simply.

In *When I Pray, What Does God Do?* David explains how for many years, many scientists and a good number of Christians have interpreted Newtonian mechanical theory in such a way that precludes the possibility of God working directly for specific purposes. Newtonian theory is based on order and predictability. This does provide space for God being the creator of the ordered systems we observe in the universe but makes it much harder, if not impossible, to attribute miraculous interventions to divine activity as clearly Luke is content to do in Acts.

David then goes on to explain how advances in chaos and quantum theories have created space for understanding the activity of God in a way denied by many interpretations of Newtonian mechanical theory. Quantum theory 'offers a tantalising pointer that relationality is part of the physicality of the world, something that is at the heart of prayer'.[9]

Meanwhile chaos theory challenges the predictability of Newtonian physics pointing out that there are systems in the universe that are extremely sensitive to initial conditions. Consequently scientists may be able to very accurately predict some events but not others.

The philosopher Karl Popper suggests that the universe contains both clocks and clouds. Clocks representing systems and events that are predictable, regular, measurable and explainable which theologically could be attributed to the initial creative work of God. Clouds, meanwhile, are irregular and may come with an element of mystery which theologically allows for God to be active and creative in the present as well as the past.

In answering the question 'When I pray, what does God do?' David Wilkinson suggests:

There is a real sense that God is doing and can do a number of things. First, God is sustaining the structure of the universe. Second, God is transforming this creation into new creation. Third, God transforms the person who prays to collaborate in building the kingdom. Fourth, God could be answering some prayers through working in the uncertainty and hidden arena of the quantum world and in chaotic systems. Fifth, God could work by transcending his normal ways of working for specific purposes.[10]

I find this very helpful as it provides a framework for understanding how signs and wonders can be both the work of a miraculous moment and the miracle of persistence. There is both scientific and theological integrity here that allows us to hold the view that God works through both the regular rhythms of creation, the faithfulness and persistence of those seeking to do God's will and specific acts of grace i.e. signs and wonders.

The Place of the Holy Habits

So how do the holy habits that we will soon explore in Part 2 relate to signs and wonders? Well our growth in holiness and fruitfulness as we practise the habits is in itself a gift of God's grace and a sign of divine activity within us. Furthermore the more we practise the holy habits the more signs and wonders we will see. All of the habits can bring forth miracles of transformation with the habit of prayer having a particular part to play. And there is no greater miracle than the transformation of a human heart.

When I worked for Ford I let it be known I was a follower of Jesus and tried my best to live a life that honoured him and blessed others, not always doing this well of course. Most colleagues were quite happy with this but there was one called Gary* who seemed to enjoy picking up on anything I did wrong and having subtle but annoying digs at my faith. I did my best to pray for Gary, that God would do something in his life.

One day it seemed as if my prayers had been answered – when Gary was transferred to another part for the company.

A few months later I, too, was transferred. To the same office that

Gary had gone to. On day one at the new office guess who was there to greet me? Fearing the worst I was stunned and amazed when Gary bounced up, greeted me warmly and said, 'Sue* and I have been thinking we would like to get our boys to explore the Christian faith. Could you recommend a good local church?'

* Not their real names.

Gladness and generosity is another of the habits that can result in some truly wonderful signs.

A group of Muslims bought a piece of land next to Heartsong Methodist Church in Memphis, Tennessee, to build a Mosque and Community Centre. The church thought hard about how to react. They put up a big notice outside telling their Muslim neighbours that they were welcome. The Muslims were so surprised and pleased they went to talk to the minister, who asked what his church could do to help them. They asked if they could rent a little room as temporary accommodation – he let them have the biggest room they had. When they had a church barbecue they bought halal meat so they could invite the Muslims. They began to work together on neighbourhood projects to help the poor.

A journalist from CNN alleged that they never published good news stories about Muslims because there aren't any. Someone challenged them to report what was happening at Heartsong so they made a 90-second video about the church which was looped on the CNN news channel over the course of a day.

A few days later the minister had a phone call from Kashmir. The caller said that he and his friends had been sitting in a café watching CNN when the story about the Muslims and the Christians came on. They were speechless when they saw it because they had been told that all Americans hated Muslims. They did not think Christians could get on with Muslims. They talked about what they could do in response to what they had seen of the Methodists at Heartsong and they decided that they should take care of the little Christian church in their community. They went and cleaned the church inside and out, washing off the offensive graffiti which had been daubed there. They made the minister a promise that, for the rest of their lives, they would take care of the Christians in their community as the people at Heartsong had taken care of their Muslim neighbours.[11]

The Wild Gospel

In her superb books, *The Wild Gospel*[12] and *Following Jesus*,[13] Alison Morgan celebrates the continuing work of the Holy Spirit in revealing signs and wonders through the prayers and actions of followers of Jesus. She presents a rich array of stories of healings, conversions and other wonderful signs of God's grace at work. The stories come from across the UK and around the world – including many stories from Africa in particular. Some of the healings she testifies to are apparently the work of a moment whilst others the result of patient faithful prayer and medical care. Amongst the latter is the story of her own husband who suffered multiple life-threatening injuries when he was struck by a lorry.[14]

Alison also tells a number of stories of people whose lives, rather like Fabrice Muamba's, are walking signs of wonder. One of those she shares also comes from the world of football.

Dave Jeal was a fan of Bristol Rovers. Unfortunately he got drawn into the dark side of the game that was prevalent in the 80s and 90s and developed a thirst for violence and hooliganism. In ever more trouble, in and out of jobs and in danger of going to prison he met a young woman who startled him by asking him to go to church with her. Naturally he declined but undeterred the plucky woman asked, 'You scared then?' Unable to decline such a challenge he went to church – and hated it. At the end of the service two brave men offered to pray with him. Dave was unsure what to do – should he give it a try or 'break this bloke's nose'. Thankfully, by the narrowest of margins he opted to give it a try. 'From that second on,' he says, 'I knew there was a God. I felt that all the anger I'd carried around all my life had been taken from me. And I thought, that is it, everything changes from here.' And it did. Today Dave is married to Nikki, a doctor, he is a pastor of a church and chaplain to his beloved Bristol Rovers Football Club.[15]

Holy Humility

We noted in Chapter 1 that when it comes to discipleship the initiative is with Jesus. It is he who calls us to the adventure of discipleship. It is he who invites us to share his life, his mission and his sufferings. When it comes to signs and wonders humility is essential. Signs and wonders are a gift of the divine community to, and sometimes through, the human community. They cannot be produced to order and the dangers of distortion, deceit and manipulation are never far away. This was brilliantly illustrated in the character Jonas Nightingale played by Steve Martin in the film *Leap of Faith*. Nightingale is a charlatan show preacher, deceiving people into believing that miraculous healings have occurred at his revival meetings. Then one night he is stunned when a young boy with a simple faith is healed; Nightingale's tricks having had nothing to do with it.

In humility we need to recognise gifts of God for what they are. In humility we also need to recognise that there is and always will be an element of mystery as to why we see some signs and not others.

Someone very close to me says that he kisses a miracle good night every night. Michael* and Anne* love being with children. Michael is a church minister and Anne is a teacher. They longed to have a child of their own but as the years went by there was no sign of a child being conceived. So the medical investigations began. Tests, exploratory operations, medication, but still no joy. One Mothering Sunday Anne was in hospital recovering from the latest exploratory procedure whilst Michael was baptising a baby. The little girl was the mother's seventh child. She was absolutely beautiful. Michael kept it together smiling and being professional but inside his heart was breaking. When everyone was gone he went to the front of the church, knelt at the communion table and cried his heart out.

A few months later a final operation had been arranged. Just three days before it was due to happen a little blue line appeared in the pregnancy test. Michael and Anne were stunned. That little blue line is now a fine young man on the threshold of a promising career and living the adventure of following Jesus for himself.

Despite all of their best efforts and much heartache Michael and Anne were not able to provide their son with a sibling. Two years ago Anne was diagnosed with a medical condition undiscovered but present all those years ago which may explain why there have been no siblings and makes that thin blue line, in Anne and Michael's eyes at least, a sign and wonder of God's grace for which they will be for ever grateful.

(This story is told with permission but to protect privacy I have changed the names).

The Greatest Sign of All

As you will gather from reading this book, one of the biggest influences on my life and thinking as a follower of Jesus is David Watson. I was privileged to be part of St Michael-le-Belfrey during David's last year there. The church itself was a sign and wonder having grown under David's leadership from a very small, elderly congregation into a six-hundred-plus fellowship of all ages. A living example of the miracle of death and resurrection, St Michael's was at the forefront of charismatic renewal attracting visitors from all over the world keen to see what God was doing.

In 1982 David left York to go to London in order to develop further his international ministry. Just a few months later he was diagnosed with cancer. Through his ministry David had prayed for and seen many people healed. He had encouraged the healing ministries of others and, in turn, was encouraged himself by others who exercised such ministries, not least his great friend John Wimber. With typical candidness David shared news of his illness and an avalanche of prayer was unleashed. John Wimber flew from America to pray for him. Other prominent Christian leaders also came to pray. In his book *Fear No Evil*[16] David talks of these prayer encounters and the grace and peace he found through many of them. He also testifies to wonderful moments during his struggles with illness. Amongst the most moving are the stories of reconciliation with others with whom relationships over the years had become strained, including a number of Christian leaders.

With his physical strength ebbing away David concluded *Fear No Evil* with these words reminiscent of Jesus in Gethsemane:

> I am ready to go and be with Christ for ever. That would be literally heaven. But I'm equally ready to stay, if that is what God wants.
>
> Father, not my will but yours be done. In that position of security I have experienced once again his perfect love, a love that casts out all fear.[17]

Late one February Friday evening David said to his wife Anne, 'I'm very tired, let's go home.' He died peacefully early the next morning.

A few weeks later I joined with thousands of others for a thanksgiving service for David at York Minster. It was not the ending many of us had hoped for and prayed for. Many questions beginning with 'why' still remained. But that day the Holy Spirit that had been so active in David's life was powerfully present in the Minster. Amidst all the sadness there was tremendous joy. Amidst all the questions there was the most profound sense of hope and assurance as we rejoiced for David in the gifts of salvation: wholeness, heaven and complete healing. The event was a celebration of the greatest sign of all, resurrection. It was quite literally wonder full.

Holy Expectation

We go now to consider how disciples of Jesus can be formed though the practising of holy habits. Let us do so open to the possibilities of all sorts of signs and wonders that bring healing, hope, new life, resurrection and reconciliation to this world that God made and loves and longs to see renewed.

For Further Reflection and Action

Personally

David Wilkinson encourages us to not make God too small, or in other words to let God be God. Take some time to quietly think this through. How open are you to God surprising you?

Is there a 'Gary' in your life? If so, keep on praying for a miracle in their life!

It may be that reading this you have been hurt by the deceitful and manipulative words or actions of someone purporting to act in the name of Jesus. If so I would encourage you to seek counsel and help.

Locally

How can your community of disciples be a sign to the wonder of God's love in your local context?

Could you offer radical generous hospitality to strangers in your community as a sign of God's Kingdom?

In these days there is a renewed openness to ministries of healing for those distressed in body, mind or spirit. Could you offer such ministry to your community through the holy habits of prayer and the breaking of bread (in the context of Holy Communion)?

Globally

Christians in other continents, Africa in particular, have different world views and understandings of signs and wonders to those in the West. Take some time to explore these, being open to learn from them. Alison Morgan's writing would help here.

Reflect on the Heartsong story. How could you be a sign and wonder of grace to a people from a different culture or context? Perhaps one that is in the majority in a country where Christians are a persecuted minority.

Biblical Passages to Reflect On
- Read through the biblical material referenced in this chapter.

What do you notice in these passages?

What will you do or change in the light of what you have read and noticed?

Recommended Reading

- James D.G. Dunn, *Jesus and the Spirit*.
- Alison Morgan, *The Wild Gospel*.
- David Wilkinson, *When I Pray, What Does God Do?*

Endnotes

1. Fabrice Muamba, *I'm Still Standing*, Liverpool: Sport Media, 2012, p9.
2. One such example follows immediately in Acts 3 with the healing of the lame man.
3. Luke 7:18–22; Acts 4: 8–14.
4. F.F. Bruce, *The Book of the Acts Revised*, Grand Rapids: Erdmans, 1988, p74. Luke 9:1–2 and 11, Luke 10:9.
5. Acts 2:43; 4:30; 5:12; 6:8; 14:3; 15:12 commented on in James D.G. Dunn, *The Acts of the Apostles* (Peterborough: Epworth, 1996), p30.
6. James D.G. Dunn, *Jesus and the Spirit*, London: SCM Press, 1975, p163.
7. Romans 15:19; 1 Corinthians 12:10, 28f; 2 Corinthians 12:12; Galatians 3:5.
8. Hebrews 2:4.
9. David Wilkinson, *When I Pray, What Does God Do?* Oxford: Monarch Books, 2015, p154.
10. Ibid, p209.
11. This story has now been written up in many places. As far as I can tell it first appeared in Jim Wallis' book *On God's Side: What Religion Forgets and Politics Hasn't Learned About Serving the Common Good*. You can also read an interview with Jim in which he quotes this story at www.yesmagazine.org/issues/love-and-the-apocalypse/jim-wallis-the-common-good-in-a-violent-world.
12. Alison Morgan, *The Wild Gospel*, Abingdon: Monarch Books, 2004.
13. Alison Morgan, *Following Jesus: The Plural of Disciple is Church*, Wells; Resource, 2015.
14. Alison Morgan, *The Wild Gospel*, Abingdon: Monarch Books, 2004, p263f.
15. Alison Morgan, *Following Jesus: The Plural of Disciple is Church*, Wells; Resource, 2015, pp67–68.
16. David Watson, *Fear No Evil*, London: Hodder and Stoughton, 1984.
17. Ibid, p171.

Part 2
The Nurture of Discipleship

6
Holy Habitats

'Discipleship flourishes in an atmosphere of grace; it withers in an environment of rules and regulations.'[1]

Jesus called his first followers into community; to be with him and to be sent out by him. To eat with him, pray with him, learn with him; to be challenged, transformed and guided; and when life and faith failed to be forgiven, restored and sent out again. Together they fed the hungry, proclaimed Good News and opened people's eyes to the much longed for Kingdom of God. They also lived sacrificially, suffered and were granted glimpses of glory.

Whenever we see the discipleship movement of Jesus being renewed we see a rediscovery of church as missional community with a renewed emphasis on both outward-looking service and inward-focused depth of relationship. We see a trinity of vital relationships reinvigorated; relationships with the divine Trinitarian community, relationships with a world in need of love and relationships with fellow disciples.

Sacramental Grace-full Community

In the early days of the Fresh Expressions movement I conducted some research to see how newly forming Christian communities were making and nurturing disciples of Jesus. Time and time again I was reminded of the value of community or holy habitat. Early fresh expressions pioneers were seeking to create communities where belonging comes before believing and which model holistic living. Communities that know the power of a rich spiritual life of prayer and worship and have a deep sense of God's immanence and transcendence. Communities that are missional and welcoming. Sacramental communities that live and model the grace of God. Prophetic communities from which grace and holiness flow as disciples grow and share in God's Kingdom mission in the world. In this sort of environment the nurturing of disciples flourishes.

Two pioneers who know the value of sacramental and prophetic community are Barbara Glasson and Ian Mobsby. When she was leading the bread-making church Somewhere Else in Liverpool, Barbara told me that they sought to make disciples 'through friendship, laughter, being real with each other, finding a way to engage in honest conversation, honouring questions, encouragement and mutual learning'. Meanwhile, when Ian was leading the new monastic community Moot he explained to me that 'grace and radical generosity are the focus of the community and its understanding of the Greek New Testament word for church, *ecclesia*'. The root meaning of ecclesia is 'gathering' and speaks of a community consciously gathering around Jesus.

Both Somewhere Else[2] and Moot[3] were, in different ways, modelling sacramental community. Community that is a visible sign and prophetic symbol of the radical grace of God.

The sacramental dynamic in fresh expressions is given practical expression through table fellowship (a holy habit we examine in Chapter 14) and a culture of hospitality. Michael Perham and Mary Gray-Reeves explore this culture in emerging churches in Britain and the United States in their inspiring book *The Hospitality of God*. Having visited fourteen fresh expressions they were both impressed by the quality of what they experienced, the care and creativity with which services were prepared and the welcoming hospitality that was offered.

Within the sacramental environment, the specific sacrament of Holy Communion is highly valued right across the ecclesiological spectrum (we explore this more fully in Chapter 10). But as Barbara Glasson explained to me, Holy Communion is so much more than a simple shared meal or a celebratory thanksgiving of the great creating and saving acts of God. At Somewhere Else, Holy Communion was not simply something they *did*; it was what they *were* – a thankful, blessed, broken and shared people.

Intentional Community

In his research into the role of small groups in forming disciples, Roger Walton concluded that there are three primary 'formative agents'[4] when it comes to nurturing disciples: mission, worship and intentional Christian community (that we explore more in Chapters 13 Service, 16 Worship and 17 Making More Disciples). This matches my findings when talking with healthy new churches around the UK. There is an intentionality about the relationships they share and the community they form.

In unpacking what he means by intentional community, Roger draws on insights offered by Dietrich Bonhoeffer in his book *Life Together*.[5] Bonhoeffer advocates the practising of a number of the holy habits including prayer, biblical teaching and eating together. But more than that it is the quality of shared life within the Christian community that is key for him.

> Living together is to enable people to become aware of their weaknesses and fantasies, practise serving and truth-telling, confront and confess sin and rely more and more on the grace of God made known in the cross. The practices are to form a people that by its life communicates the gospel.[6]

Bonhoeffer identifies five ministries that are essential within intentional

Christian Community. Ministries of

- Holding one's tongue.
- Meekness.
- Listening.
- Helpfulness.
- Bearing with others individuality, weaknesses and oddities.

There is a wonderful sense of down-to-earth, counter-cultural holiness here.

It is easy to romanticise Christian community. To paint an idyllic picture of harmony and tranquillity. The reality is often far from idyllic. As one minister said to me recently, maintaining harmony and commonality of purpose is 'bloody hard work'. Truth be told it has always been that way – just read Acts and the epistles of Paul. The very first Christian community comprised of the twelve disciples gathered around Jesus had some wonderful moments of missional effectiveness and glorious transcendent worship. They saw all sorts of signs and wonders, and experienced a depth of fellowship almost beyond imagining. Yet because they were human and because they were works in progress, they argued and bickered. They jockeyed for position and got carried away on ego trips. And they had Jesus physically present with them.

Most sadly of all, when it came to the crunch and the hour of Jesus' greatest need, they betrayed, denied and abandoned him. But Jesus did not deny or abandon them. After the resurrection he called them again to be with him, and to be sent by him. To be sacramental community. A grace-full sign of the Kingdom. Flawed human beings being transformed by the life-giving love of God.

The Value of the Small

The re-emergence of attention to intentional community should not surprise us. Time and again when we see the church renewed in mission and discipleship we see a renewed emphasis on and commitment to intentional, supportive and accountable relationships.

It is a common characteristic of healthy churches that they have small groups and for many they are both the prime expression of church and the place through which growth in discipleship is encouraged. Jeremy Parkes, the pastor of Living Hope Church, a young and vibrant church in Dudley says, 'We are not a church with small groups, we are a church of small groups.'[7]

In the early church, followers of Jesus were formed in small groups known as the *catechumenate* for a period of two or three years before they were baptised and became full members of the church. These periods of intense apprenticeship recreating the experience of the first disciples with Jesus.

From the fourth century onwards, as part of the monastic movement communities of Christians seeking a radically different lifestyle formed residential communities to seek God and live counter-culturally. These communities evolved habits and patterns of life together, from which they lived missionally.

Jumping on in time to the post reformation period we find a new emphasis on groups of Christians meeting together for informal learning and fellowship. The home was emphasised by the likes of Richard Baxter in his manual *The Reformed Pastor* and by the Moravian communities.

Early Methodism was rooted in small groups known as Class Meetings which were means of community and discipleship for the many new Christians who formed the early Methodist societies. These meetings were based on the principles of mutual accountability and were at the heart of the missionary movement. They were mirrored in parts of other British churches in what were called 'cottage meetings' for prayer and study in the eighteenth and nineteenth centuries.

Around the world intentional community has been at the heart of a number of fruitful discipleship movements including Cell Church[8] which originated in Korea, Base Ecclesial Communities[9] born in Latin America and Covenant Discipleship Groups[10] from North America which provide a contemporary application of the discipleship model so effectively developed by John Wesley.

A Range of Holy Habitats

Holy habitats are needed and form in a variety of places and contexts – not just in gatherings that we call church. Roger Walton highlights the L'Arche communities founded by Jean Vanier – where people with various abilities and disabilities live together in Christian community – and hospices as examples of holy habitats or intentional community 'built in different ways on the stories of Jesus'.[11]

In his book *Being Church, Doing Life*, Mike Moynagh argues passionately for the formation of what he calls Gospel Communities in workplaces in particular but also in places of socialisation and leisure. Such communities have two core purposes: a primary purpose of mission – modelling and proclaiming the kingdom by example; and a secondary purpose of fellowship and nurture.

I know the value of being part of a small Christian community at work from my own time as a financial analyst and young adult working for Ford Motor Company. The help I gained in seeking to live out my discipleship in an authentic, down-to-earth, holy way was invaluable. As was the wisdom I gained in bearing witness to Jesus with confidence and credibility. To this day one of my most valued possessions is the card I was given when I left Ford to train for the ministry. They may just have been glad to see me go, of course, but the warmth of good wishes from colleagues is something I will treasure for ever. It was as if they saw me as their gift to the church. 'Your move from Ford to the Lord is one I will feel very much,' wrote one colleague who I had prayed for and supported through a series of tribulations. The poetry is great in that quote but the theology is dodgy, for the Lord did not leave Ford when I did. I see my time there as being as much a part of my ministry as the subsequent time I have had as an ordained church minister. In fact I often miss the down-to-earth honesty of the Ford offices and evenings in the pub.

Many church schools and a good number of state schools led by Christian head teachers are exemplary models of holy habitats: introducing children and young people to Jesus, teaching them to pray, opening the Bible together, serving the needy and living by Christ-like values.

The Home and Family

Christian Communities were first formed in homes. By the end of the New Testament period the home was still the normative gathering place for Christians seeking to form holy habitats of mission and discipleship. Within those homes, the household or extended family was itself a community of followers of Jesus.

As far back as 1983 David Prior was urging a rediscovery of the home as a place of discipleship formation, calling for a new movement of 'grassroots communities'. Prior was inspired by simple but dynamic Christian communities, especially those in Latin America that know how to truly be evangelical i.e. truly good news.

> Other churches may be richer in institutions, or talk more about the Gospel. But the grassroots communities are more evangelical because of the evangelical notes of joy, hope, enthusiasm, joviality, largeness of heart, good news despite oppression. [12]

There is a lot to be said for simplicity, and part of the genius of the holy habits is that they can be practised in any culture, community or context by people of all ages and abilities. David Prior commenting on the emerging grass roots communities of Central and South America put it this way:

> The new figure of the church is born when poor and unprepossessing groups of Christians gather together, even under a mango tree, to pray, to hear the Gospel, to witness to their faith in Jesus and to follow Him.'[13]

We noted earlier the genius of John Wesley in nurturing disciples through small intentional communities or class groups. It is arguable that at least some of this genius was inherited directly from or by watching his formidable mother Susannah who made their home a fertile discipleship environment for young 'Jack' and his eighteen(!) siblings, regularly practising with them the holy habits of prayer and biblical teaching in particular.

Over the years, in the West at least, there has been a tendency to subcontract out the discipleship of our families believing it to be the job of the church or the youth group to nurture and grow people (especially children and young people) in Christian life and holy habits. Such an approach is unbiblical and there is an urgent need to reclaim the home and family as intentional Christian communities.

Lucy Moore, the founder of the phenomenon that is Messy Church, is strongly advocating the rediscovery of the home and family as discipleship communities. In his excellent book *Making Disciples in Messy Church*, Paul Moore (Lucy's husband) laments the lack of attention given to the holy habits of discipleship in many Christian homes, pointing out that when asked how those who grew up in Christian homes knew it was a Christian home most people say 'because we went to church'. He then goes on to say:

> Messy Church wants to encourage parents to take back the responsibility for the spiritual formation of their children by equipping them to explore faith and grow in discipleship along with their children. Families require support in order to learn the skills they need to live the Christian life and to pass those skills on to future generations.[14]

Companions on the Journey

In addition to the community experience of groups (something we will return to when we look at the holy habit of fellowship in Chapter 9), there are a range of relationships that are conducive to growth as we seek to develop in our own discipleship and help to nurture others.

First of all there are crowds – big gatherings where we can lose ourselves and experience in a gloriously ironic way a form of intimacy with the divine community of Father, Son and Holy Spirit that is difficult to know in smaller groups. Sometimes it is energising and helpful just to get 'lost in wonder, love and praise'[15] without having to discuss it or give an account of how we feel to someone else. Celebrations, cathedrals and festivals are all helpful in this regard.

At the opposite end of the scale are a number of helpful one-to-one relationships. For those new to the adventure of discipleship, one-to-one mentoring or apprenticing relationships can be particularly helpful. A good biblical model for this is provided by Paul and Timothy. This is especially valuable when someone new to the faith is paired with someone who has been journeying with Jesus for some time. It is important that these relationships are ones of mutual learning. When I was researching discipleship in fresh expressions, Andrew Jones from Grace Church, Hackney explained their approach to me:

> We try and pair up people in discipleship relationships. They typically meet once a week to read the Bible together, pray and talk about issues they face. It's usually a more mature Christian meeting with a new or not-yet Christian. The shape of the relationship is worked out by the pair.

Others intentionally meet with a Spiritual Director or Soul Friend – someone with whom they can talk in absolute confidence about their discipleship, benefitting from the wisdom and experience that the director or friend has accumulated from their own discipleship adventure.

And then there are those who could be called Companions on the Way. This is another biblical form of relationship encouraged by Jesus who sent out the twelve[16] and then the seventy[17] on the adventure of discipleship, two by two. Perhaps the most famous New Testament story of two companions walking together is the story known as the Emmaus Road[18] when Jesus becomes known to Cleopas and his companion through the holy habits of opening the Scriptures and breaking bread.

Significantly in the context of thinking about discipleship, the English word 'companion' is derived from two Latin words – *cum panis* – and literally means a person with whom one breaks bread. For Roger Walton,

Companionship is the essence of what it means to be a Christian disciple. We are called to the journey of faith in God, and we are blessed to have fellow travellers. These are not simply people going the same way, a parallel path, each following Jesus. We are given to and for each other to be channels of grace and agents of formation for one another. Even as we are formed and transformed in mission, worship and community, we are set alongside each other needing the gifts and graces, the insights and experiences of our sisters and brothers. Sometimes our companions will be in our home among our families, sometimes wise counsellors, experienced mentors or spiritual friends. Often they will not be identified in any of these categories, but our journeying with them will nevertheless enable us to learn from God and grow to be more Christlike.[19]

A Shared Adventure

So the adventure of discipleship is a shared journey made personally and collectively in response to the call of Jesus. A journey made in the company of the divine community of Father, Son and Holy Spirit; and of our fellow disciples gathered by Jesus to be his body on earth today and sent by him to continue his Kingdom mission.

As we gather in twos, small groups or big crowds, and as we scatter and go to serve where we are sent we are nurtured by and live out the holy habits to which we now turn.

Suggestions for Further Reflection and Action

Personally
With whom do you share a companion relationship as a disciple of Jesus? If the answer is 'no one' ask the Spirit to show you who you could develop a companion relationship with.

How might your home be more intentionally a holy habitat? And what about your workshop, day centre, office, staff room or other place of work or meeting?

Locally
How fully and effectively is your local church or fellowship group a visible sign and prophetic symbol of the radical grace of God?

How effective are your small groups? Do they need to be renewed? Do they need to be formed?

Globally
There is a risk when relationships are deep that they become exclusive. In your companion conversations be disciplined in including conversations about people/needs/issues beyond yourselves. Talk about and pray for those in the news and the needs and joys of disciples around the world.

Do the same in your small and larger groups and gatherings. When you pray the Lord's Prayer be conscious of the Kingdom petition being a prayer for the Kingdom to come on all of the earth.

Biblical Passages to Reflect On
• Luke 24:13–32 and Acts 16:25–34

What do you notice in these passages?

What will you do or change in the light of what you have read and noticed?

Recommended Reading
• Paul Moore, *Making Disciples in Messy Church*.

- Alison Morgan, *Following Jesus: The Plural of Disciple is Church.*
- David Prior, *The Church in the Home.*

Endnotes

7
Introducing the Holy Habits

They devoted themselves to the apostles' teaching and fellowship, to the breaking of bread and the prayers. Awe came upon everyone, because many wonders and signs were being done by the apostles. All who believed were together and had all things in common; they would sell their possessions and goods and distribute the proceeds to all, as any had need. Day by day, as they spent much time together in the temple, they broke bread at home and ate their food with glad and generous hearts, praising God and having the goodwill of all the people. And day by day the Lord added to their number those who were being saved.

Acts 2:42–47

In six succinct verses Luke paints a vivid portrait of the community of disciples in Jerusalem following the ascension of Jesus and the outpouring of the Spirit at Pentecost. 'A beautiful cameo of the Spirit-filled church.'[1] The mood is one of adventure and excitement and the atmosphere is eschatological (that big word again) with the outpouring of the Spirit being seen as a sign of the immanence of the Kingdom.[2]

In the previous chapter we noted the importance of community. It is in community that we practise the holy habits of discipleship, being nurtured in them so that we may live them out in our day-to-day lives wherever God calls and sets us. Community is important for Luke and in this passage he presents an exemplary model. As C.K. Barrett comments:

> Luke wished his readers to see what the life of the Christians was like in the apostolic period in order that they might imitate it . . . His story is not simply a series of biographies but the story of a community.[3]

A community centred on the now risen and ascended Jesus and growing out of a shared experience of the Spirit.[4] A community characterised by ten holy habits. According to James Dunn this form of Christ-centred, Spirit-filled discipleship community reappears whenever the discipleship movement of Jesus is renewed. Commenting on Acts 2 he says:

> The portrayal may be somewhat idealized . . . But anyone who is familiar with movements of enthusiastic spiritual renewal will recognise authentic notes: the enthusiasm of the members of the renewal group, with a sense of overflowing joy, desire to come together frequently, eating together and worshipping and including the readiness for unreserved commitment to one another in a shared common life.[5]

Divine and Down to Earth

The habits we find being practised in Acts 2 are simultaneously divine and down to earth, godly and human. An expression, outworking or sign of the two great acts of God: creation and salvation. They are life-giving and loving. Brought to new life by the Spirit they are as ancient as the Old Testament with examples of and allusions to the habits to be found throughout the story of the pilgrim people of God.

The habits are truly ecumenical and suitable for Christians of all streams, denominations, traditions and nationalities. From Jerusalem to Judea, Samaria and on to the ends of the earth[6] they travel well. Buzz Aldrin even practised the habits of reading the Bible and breaking bread in the Lunar Lander on the surface of the moon.[7]

Beautiful in their simplicity, the habits can be practised in any culture, context and community, by those of all ages and abilities. When asked how others could start a fresh expression of church, teenager Lucy at The Bridge in Hinckley said, 'Talk together, eat together, pray together.'[8] Luke would like that.

So holy habits are not a fad or a trendy new initiative but ancient yet ever fresh Spirit-filled, Christ-centred disciplines of discipleship that nurture us individually and collectively as we journey on the adventure of discipleship to see Kingdom transformation in the world God loves and in our lives too. In short, holy habits are a way of life.

The Value of the Habitual

We noted earlier how the root meaning of the word disciple is one who learns as they follow. We learn a lot from the habits we practise. We are formed and transformed by them. The golfer Gary Player at the height of his success was once asked why he was so lucky. He famously answered that the more he practised the luckier he got.

One of my guilty secrets is that I am an Aston Villa fan. Villa seemingly always lose to Manchester United. One day I realised why. Whilst they were warming up United practised over and over again their attacking routines until they were intuitive. As if by telepathy the players knew where each other were and where the ball was going. Come the match itself United scored with a pattern of play that was virtually an identical replica of the patterns they had practised before the game.

Discipleship is first, foremost and above all else a calling. But is also a way of life that flourishes as we practise holy habits. As we practise them, so Christ-like character grows. Graham Cray puts it this way:

There are things Christians need to learn, but more important still, though not separate from learning the faith, is what Christians have to become. Character formation is the object of disciple making. It is achieved through habit, through godly repetition. It involves spiritual disciplines, but also daily obedience to the way of Christ.[9]

Graham goes on to say that 'this sort of character formation has a much greater chance of success in community'.[10]

Mike Moynagh agrees with this saying that 'Christian character grows when the individual learns empowered habits'[11] before affirming the role of community in forming these habits. For Graham Tomlin a disciple shaped by holy habits will demonstrate a quality of life that overflows with Christ-like character:

> A mature Christian is someone in whom a quality of life has grown that enables her to be generous even when she is poor, to love until it hurts, to show kindness as a regular habit of life, without even thinking about it.[12]

Keeping On

On the adventure of discipleship we are blessed with moments of great joy, mountain-top experiences that excite and energise us. We thank God for such moments and sometimes, often maybe, wish that life could be like that all the time. Like Peter who wanted to build dwellings on the Mount of Transfiguration[13] we can want to capture the highs and live continually at that level. But life and discipleship are not like that.

Simon Guillebaud affirms this in his stimulating book *More Than Conquerors* which reads at times like the Action Man guide to discipleship. He says:

> When it comes to our spiritual lives, we can't be dependent on 'highs' engendered through large meetings or conferences, because our lives are not lived out on a daily basis at such venues. We need to nurture our relationship with Christ through disciplined times of regular intimacy.

Simon highlights the importance of hanging on in there and the value of 'plodding perseverance'.

The value of practising holy habits is realised most deeply when life gets tough. In times of struggle and suffering the simple disciplines that we will explore are life-giving and lifesaving. They help us to experience the grace under pressure that Paul testifies to in Romans 8 and 2 Corinthians 4: 'We are afflicted in every way, but not crushed; perplexed, but not driven to despair; persecuted, but not forsaken; struck down, but not destroyed.'[14]

When the Archbishop of Canterbury's Middle Eastern envoy Terry Waite was taken captive in the Lebanese city of Beirut he was held in the most horrendous of conditions, often on his own in terms of human companionship. In his book *Taken on Trust* he shares the story of a Christmas celebration that he experienced at midnight on Christmas Eve in his cell a few miles from where 'Jesus was born on this holy night'.[15] As he read the Gospel of John the words of the prologue came alive with a profound poignancy. 'The light shines in the darkness . . . and we beheld his glory . . . full of grace and truth'.[16] Jesus was with him in the darkness. He prayed, broke bread and celebrated a simple Holy Communion with bread and water.

The presence of Christ and his practising of simple holy habits sustained him through those hellish days of captivity. As did the fruit of others practising simple holy habits many miles away.

On arriving back in Britain after his release Terry gave an impromptu speech in which he thanked those who 'kept us alive in their prayers, in their thoughts and their actions',[17] expressing their concern for the Kingdom values of 'justice, peace and truth'. He particularly thanked the person who had simply but generously sent him a postcard that had somehow made its way to him which said, 'We remember you, we shall not forget, we shall continue to pray for you, and to work for all people who are detained around the world.'[18]

As we practise the holy habits simply and faithfully, we may never know the full extent of what they achieve in blessing others and building the Kingdom of God.

Living Rhythmically

In recent years there has been a rediscovery of the value of rules or rhythms of life: patterns of prayer and regular practice of the other holy habits that deepen our dwelling in Christ and equip us in our day-to-day lives as Kingdom-focused missionary disciples in the various contexts that we serve.

Many rhythms of life are developed more fully to be rules of life that encapsulate commitment and incorporate values as well as practices. Pete Greig, the founder of the 24-7 prayer movement which is committed to regular prayer and active Christian service, suggests: 'A rule of life is a set of principles and practices we build into the rhythm of our daily lives, helping us to deepen our relationship with God and to serve him more faithfully.'[19]

Rhythms of life can be very simple. The Hebrew prophet Micah provides a famous early example:

> What does the LORD require of you but to do justice, and to love kindness, and to walk humbly with your God?[20]

Or they can be more sophisticated and nuanced to the ethos of a particular group of disciples. The Venture FX pioneers, an evolving missional community within the Methodist Church, has adopted this as a rhythm of life:

> We are committed to a rhythm of life which flows from three core values:
> • Innovation: breaking new ground and planting for the future.
> • Imagination: dreaming God's vision for what church could become.
> • Incarnation: immersed in our communities in the name of Christ.
>   We seek to express those values by:
> • Daily reflecting on our spiritual journey as disciples of Jesus.

- Weekly observing a common day for the discipline of prayer and fasting.
- Monthly gathering together for support, encouragement and learning.
- Annually sharing in a retreat to renew our individual and common life with God.[21]

There are a wealth of helpful writings and resources around rhythms and rules of life. If you would like to explore these more there are suggestions at the end of the chapter.

A Profundity of Habits

The ten holy habits that we explore in this book are not offered as an exclusive list. Why ten? Because that is the number that I have identified in Acts 2:42–47 and, as the quote from James Dunn at the beginning of the chapter makes clear, these core habits recur time and again when the discipleship movement of Jesus is renewed by the Spirit and re-energised for life and mission.

The habits explored are inter-related. They will be presented individually but together they form an holistic way of life for both the individual disciple of Jesus and the Christian community of which they are part.

There are many other habits that we could add both from biblical material and from the writings of others. Some of these will be mentioned in the ten habits we do explore as they are intimately related to, or expressions of, them. A longer list of holy habits could include fasting, meditation and pilgrimage. We could add stillness and resting, celebration and play – the latter a habit of discipleship that Messy Church has brought back to the fore. And then there are prophetic witness, campaigning and friendship.

Other writers stress the value of habitual virtues. Ian Adams highlights the value of poverty (or simplicity), chastity (or fidelity) and obedience.[22] In his classic book *Celebration of Discipline*,[23] Richard Foster presents a mixture of twelve habits and values categorised into three groups:

1. Inward Disciplines: meditation, prayer, fasting and study.
2. Outward Disciplines: simplicity, solitude, submission and service.
3. Corporate Disciplines: confession, worship, guidance and celebration.

Writing more recently Graham Tomlin uses two different categories:

1. Disciplines of Abstinence: solitude, silence, fasting, frugality, chastity, secrecy and sacrifice.
2. Disciplines of Engagement: study, worship, celebration, service, prayer, fellowship, confession and submission.

Graham suggests that 'each of the classic Christian disciplines helps to develop Christian virtues reflecting the character of God in Christ'.[24]

Holy Devotion

The commitment we saw at the lakeside as the first disciples embarked on the adventure of following Jesus is apparent again in Luke's presentation of the life of the post Pentecost Christian community. 'They devoted themselves,' he says before introducing the ten holy habits that we now explore: biblical teaching, fellowship, breaking of bread, prayer, giving, service, eating together, gladness and generosity, worship and making more disciples.

Suggestions for Further Reflection and Action

Personally

Take a little time to reflect on the patterns of your life. Do you have a sense of rhythm or is everything a bit haphazard? How might a rhythm of life help you to live more effectively the adventure of discipleship?

Please see below for suggestions on where to go to develop thinking about a rhythm or rule of life.

Locally

Picture your local Christian community (if it is helpful do this literally by painting, drawing or modelling). How does your picture compare to Luke's portrayal of the first Christian community. Are there habits that compare well? Which habits compare less well? Note these for particular reflection as you read the following chapters.

Globally

What could you learn about rhythm of life from other countries and cultures? Particularly those which may be poorer financially but are more appreciative of time.

Pray for those being held captive or being persecuted in other ways who, like Terry Waite, when in captivity have to survive practising habits they have memorised.

A Biblical Passage to Reflect On

• Micah 6:6–8

What do you notice in this passage?

What will you do or change in the light of what you have read and noticed?

Recommended Reading

To explore more fully the challenge and joy of faithfully living out discipleship in everyday life I recommend Paula Gooder's excellent book *Everyday God*.

If you would like to explore further rhythms or rules of life, or create one for yourself or your community, here are some helpful resources:

- Ian Adams, *Cave, Refectory, Road*, Chapter 6.
- Ian Mobsby and Mark Berry, *A New Monastic Handbook*, Chapters 4 and 5.
- Robert Wicks, *Everyday Simplicity*.
- 24-7prayer.com/communities/practices
- Contemplative Fires' rhythm of life at freshexpressions.org.uk/stories/contemplativefire
- methodist.org.uk/media/831306/dd-explore-devotion-writing-a rule-of-life-0313.pdf

Endnotes

1. John R.W. Stott, *The Message of Acts*, Leicester: IVP, 1990, p81.
2. Acts 1:6–8.
3. C.K. Barrett, Acts 1–14, ICC, Edinburgh: T&T Clark, 2004, p160.
4. James D.G. Dunn, *The Acts of the Apostles*, Peterborough: Epworth, 1996, p35.
5. Ibid, p34.
6. Acts 1:8.
7. Buzz Aldrin, *Magnificent Desolation*, London: Bloomsbury, 2009, p26.
8. Norman Ivison, *expressions: the dvd – 1: stories of church for a changing culture*, London: Church House Publishing, 2006, Ch 13. Or freshexpressions.org.uk/resources/dvd1/13.
9. Graham Cray, Ian Mobsby and Aaron Kennedy, *New Monasticism as Fresh Expression of Church*, Norwich: Canterbury Press, 2010, p5.
10. Ibid.
11. Michael Moynagh, *Being Church, Doing Life*, Oxford: Monarch Books, 2014, p186.
12. Graham Tomlin, Spiritual Fitness, London: Continuum, 2006, p45.
13. Matthew 17:1–13; Mark 9:2–13; Luke 9:28–36.
14. 2 Corinthians 4:8–9.
15. Terry Waite, *Taken on Trust*, London: Hodder and Stoughton, 1993, p259.
16. John 1:5; 1:14
17. Terry Waite, *Taken on Trust*, London: Hodder and Stoughton, 1993, p360.
18. Ibid.
19. Pete Greig, *The Vision and the Vow*, Eastbourne: Kingsway, 2005.
20. Micah 6:8.
21. methodist.org.uk/media/636034/venturefx-rhythm-of-life-0912.pdf.

22. Ian Adams, *Cave, Refectory, Road*, Norwich: Canterbury Press, 2010, chapters 8, 9 and 10.

23. Richard Foster, *Celebration of Discipline*, London: Hodder and Stoughton, 1989.

24. Graham Tomlin, *Spiritual Fitness*, London: Continuum, 2006, p137.

8
Biblical Teaching

They devoted themselves to the apostles' teaching.
Acts 2:42

At my favourite fresh expression, Zac's Place that we visited in Chapter 3, there is a sign next to the entrance that is refreshingly different. It says: no drugs, no guns and no explosives. Immediately you get the sense that this is going to be a lively place. And then what do you find at the heart of the community? An open Bible, as Sean Stillman explains:

> Building disciples is an unbelievably messy process and I think it was messy for Jesus and it continues to be so for us. We unashamedly focus a lot of attention to studying the Bible together; we call it our Tribal Gathering. We attract all sorts, we do some good old-fashioned Bible study topped and tailed with a prayer.[1]

The first holy habit to be mentioned in Acts 2:42 has always been at the heart of healthy discipleship formation and continues to be so today.

The Apostles Teaching

The opening chapters of Acts present a continuum of ministry from Jesus through the apostles. Jesus had a teaching ministry which was rooted in the Hebrew Scriptures (the Old Testament of the Christian Bible). This is continued through those who were first identified as his disciples. Luke is not explicit about the content of the apostles' teaching in verse 42 but James Dunn argues that:

> The apostles are the medium and the guarantors of the teaching focused on fresh interpretations of the Scriptures and beginning to order the memories of Jesus' teaching and ministry into forms suitable for instruction, worship and proclamation.[2]

So the teaching is *biblical* teaching drawing on the Hebrew Scriptures, out of which Jesus taught, and Jesus' own teaching, much of which went on to be recorded in the New Testament.

Santos Yao agrees that Luke does not specify the content of the teaching but argues that this 'must have included the kerygma [proclamation] concerning the work, words and promises of Jesus.'[3] Acts 4:32 highlights the importance of the resurrection of Jesus in the teaching of the apostles.

Luke mentions the devotion of the early followers of Jesus to the apostles teaching immediately after his account of Peter's Pentecost sermon[4] – a sermon which itself is full of biblical material.[5] So in the beginning Spirit-filled, biblically-based, Christ-centred preaching was an effective way of practising the holy habit of biblical teaching. When done well it remains so today in a range of cultures and contexts. For example, many churches with a large number of students still find this way of engaging with biblical teaching to be fruitful and effective. Matt, an economics student at Birmingham University, is part of a church that places a high value on biblical teaching. Amidst all the challenges, opportunities and choices of early adulthood, he values the clarity and sense of direction he receives from the biblical teaching of the church. He says:

As we look in more depth at the Bible, we grow in understanding of what is involved with, and what it means to be, a follower of Jesus. This can then be explored and applied to our lives as we seek to live faithfully as followers of Jesus in multi-cultural universities balancing commitments of studies, sports and societies.

Learning Together

Preaching is by no means the only way to practise the habit of biblical teaching. Jesus himself preached to large gatherings but also spent much of his time facilitating teaching and learning in community, gathered in smaller groups.

Australian New Testament lecturer Sylvia Wilkey-Collinson has studied the rabbinical teaching methods of Jesus in depth. Drawing on that study and her knowledge of good adult teaching practises she advocates a 'Discipling Model of Teaching' for the fruitful nurture of disciples today.[6] Her model has six key components. It is:

1. Relational.
2. Intentional (all members have a responsibility for learning).
3. Mainly informal and life related.
4. Typically communal.
5. Reciprocal (learning is mutual and collaborative).
6. Centrifugal in focus (disciples go out from community to be involved in service and mission and then return to reflect).[7]

Whilst not disputing Paul's view that some are graced with a particular gift of teaching[8] Sylvia strongly affirms the view that teaching and learning are gifts of the whole community.

Although some may have a gift of teaching which they frequently use . . . all members of the community have a responsibility for enriching and contributing to the up-building of others. This is achieved in part by the exercise of their spiritual gifts and the example of their faithful, Christ-like living. Learning thus becomes a mutual, collaborative affair.[9]

Commenting on the text at the beginning of this chapter Loveday Alexander affirms several of the components in the Wilkey-Collinson model. Noting the coupling of the apostles' teaching and fellowship, Loveday argues that 'students learn from each other just as much as from their teachers'.[10]

Here we see the value of a blending of several of the holy habits. Biblical teaching is particularly effective when practised in the context of the kind of fellowship that we shall explore in the next chapter. It can also be augmented by the habit of eating together. Many café churches have discovered the value of exploring biblical teaching in the relaxed and open atmosphere created by the joy of sharing food. The Bible Society itself has recognised this and developed a range of resources called *Lyfe*[11] that can be used to explore biblical teaching in the café culture.

Creative Teaching and Learning

As we explore the holy habits a recurring theme will be the importance and value of connecting with the creativity of God as we practise them. I often ask groups of people to tell me what God is like. Almost always the first answer is 'loving' – appropriately enough. We then go through a range of other good answers before, on usually about the twelfth occasion, someone shouts out 'creative'. I find this intriguing as it is the first thing we know about God in the Bible. I sometimes wonder if it is the forgotten attribute of the divine community. If so, we need to keep on rediscovering it and reconnecting with it. And this applies to our practices of biblical teaching as much as anything else.

Thankfully there are many who are helping us with this. The practices of Godly Play,[12] developed by Jerome Berryman, have helped many to a refreshing engagement with biblical teaching. The Messy Church[13] movement has connected with godly creativity in all sorts of imaginative ways, bringing biblical teaching alive for children and adults alike. Many fresh expressions are exploring biblical teaching in creative ways.

When he was leading Sanctus 1 in Manchester, pioneering minister Ben Edson told me about a young man who started coming along to some of their gatherings. Quite frankly he looked bored and disengaged with what was going on. Then at one session clay was brought in and members of the community were invited to engage with the biblical text they were exploring by sculpting their response. Now such an invitation would be my worst nightmare – I have the artistic skills of an inebriated orangutan – but this young man was extremely creative and loved sculpting. At that moment the Bible came alive for him and as he moulded the clay so the Spirit got to work in his life, breathing through the text he was engaged with.

All of these creative ways of engaging with biblical teaching take seriously the diverse ways in which adults, young people and children learn. Some of us are visual learners, others primarily auditory, whilst still others learn best kinaesthetically. Jesus himself made use of all of the senses when teaching. Bereft of PowerPoint he painted vivid pictures to stimulate the visual imagination of those listening. His stories were rich in characters and evocative images. His frequent allusions to nature connected with creation and the senses of sound, touch and taste. As we practise the holy habit of biblical teaching in community it is vital that we do so in diverse ways that allow as many as possible to participate. It's about being imaginative.

This also applies to our own personal engagement with biblical teaching. As with all of the holy habits it is important to keep our practices fresh and alive. In my own following of Jesus I have used and enjoyed a variety of ways of engaging with the Bible. There have been many seasons in which I have been helped by daily Bible notes. At other times I have simply read portions of Scripture and quietly asked the Spirit to speak to me through them. Sometimes this has been augmented by the process of *lectio divina* – an ancient practice that has been brought back to prominence by the new monastic movement. It involves reading a page slowly three times.[14] After the first reading I spend a few moments in silent reflection. After the second reading I notice any words or phrases that particularly stand out. After the third reading I explore with the Spirit what this word or phrase might mean for me, those I pray for and the wider world. So the biblical teaching explored through the reading leads to prayer and action.

In addition to the above I have found daily Bible and prayer websites helpful. Then to my surprise there have been times when I have enjoyed using the creative colouring resources produced by Mary Fleeson at Lindisfarne Scriptorium[15] to reflect on a range of biblical passages.

Basildon Bound

When it comes to the holy habit of biblical teaching, community and creativity are vital. So, too, is context. *Where* we are, as well as *who* we are, affects how we engage with the Bible and how the Bible engages with us.

When I was student at York I got a summer job with Ford Motor Company at their research centre in Basildon. Moving from the beauty of the historic northern city to the concrete jungle of the new town was a big culture shock.[16] The shock was accentuated by my accommodation. A rented room on a needy estate. Whilst there I discovered that my landlady, who drank bottles of whisky at an alarming rate, had done time for violent robbery and assault. Another lodger was arrested for drug dealing and a few doors away someone was shot on their doorstep in a domestic dispute.

In York, caught up in the excitement of the charismatic renewal, I was gobbling up the biblical teaching of people like David Watson and Graham Cray, full of stories of heroes of the faith and the Spirit's gifts and work. In exile in Basildon, very different parts of the Bible came alive. Stories of God's care, cries of lament and especially the psalmists imploring prayer 'How long?' were precious gifts to a boy far from home. Psalm 40, so beautifully interpreted by U2 in their song '40' became a real source of strength.

As a keen young Christian I tried my best to pray for those around me and to share my faith. At the end of the summer I bought my landlady a Bible and presented it to her as a gift. When I got back to York a letter arrived from Basildon, written in biro on a piece of paper torn from a spiral-bound notepad, saying thank you so much for the Bible – the first book the lady had ever been given. A gift that had given her comfort and hope.

Lived-out Teaching – Purposeful and Prophetic

For Jesus it was the living-out of his teaching – teaching that was rooted in his own living-out of the Hebrew Bible – that really mattered.[17] Living it out in transformed character and Kingdom activity, in generosity, compassion and joy. The great biblical scholar Walter Brueggemann points out the importance of living out the teaching of the Bible in 'glad obedience' in the world that 'is the venue for God's reign.'[18] He advocates the living-out of biblical teaching as 'a bodily act of obedience to God-given possibility' pointing out that 'What counts in the end is not a better understanding or a new idea; what counts [for Christian disciples] is a community of engagement that takes up the gift of transformation and acts it out in the world'[19] in holy living and prophetic witness.

So, if like me you still need the index to find the book of Obadiah, and you can't quote all of Philippians off by heart, fear not. The Bible is not a book to be learnt by rote but a living story that we are invited to learn from, enter into and be shaped by so that we, in turn, may be God's agents of holiness and transformation in the world he loves.

Practising biblical living that flows from biblical teaching has led to great acts and movements of Kingdom transformation, social holiness and justice through such great figures as William Booth, Caroline Chisholm, Martin Luther King, Hannah More, Mother Teresa and William Wilberforce.

Entrepreneurial Christians in business have shown that one can be faithful, ethical and successful by living out biblical teaching. Just fifteen miles away from where I live is the Ironbridge Gorge, the birthplace of the Industrial Revolution. Visiting the homes of the Darby family, who were arguably the key players in the revolution, it is striking how their engagement with biblical teaching as part of their Quaker faith shaped the way they lived and worked in a way that gained the admiration and respect of those who worked with them and for them. Fifteen miles in the opposite direction is the village of Bournville where the story is celebrated of another Quaker family that lived by the teaching of their Bibles – the Cadburys.

Being faithful to biblical teaching has also produced some of the most moving, inspiring and challenging stories of personal courage, dignity, grace, holiness and heroism. One such story is that of Solomon Northup, powerfully portrayed in the Oscar-winning film *12 Years a Slave*. A film which also serves as a stark reminder of the horrors that can result from the abuse of biblical teaching with the slave owners taking isolated texts out of context and using them to justify their abusive, vile and evil behaviour.

Your Word is a Lamp to my Feet and a Light to my Path[20]

Amongst all the holy habits, biblical teaching has a particular part to play in forming us and guiding us on the adventure of discipleship. In his beautiful book *Everyday Simplicity* Robert Wicks says:

> Scripture helps diminish the distance between God and us because we are part of the story. Ironically scriptures are not irrelevant because they were inspired and written in the past, rather they are eternally relevant because they help us see beyond our current frame of reference which may have trapped us.

Biblical teaching draws us to Jesus – the one who calls us to follow. Jesus, the word made flesh[21] who lived by the teachings of the Hebrew Scriptures and became the centre of the teachings of the New Testament. Towards the end of his Gospel John says:

> *Now Jesus did many other signs in the presence of his disciples, which are not written in this book. But these are written so that you may come to believe that Jesus is the Messiah, the Son of God, and that through believing you may have life in his name.*[22]

Breathed through by the breath of God[23] biblical teaching nourishes us, challenges us, shapes and inspires us. It provides the reference points by which we form, evaluate and practise all of the other habits. It is a core practice.

Suggestions for Further Reflection and Action

Personally

Take some time to review your personal practice of engaging with the Bible. Is it in need of refreshing? Would a season engaging with the Bible in a different way be helpful?

One tool that you might like to explore is ORID. Originally developed by the Canadian Institute for Cultural Affairs it can be adapted to engage with biblical teaching. So:

- Observe. What do you notice in the text that you are reading?
- Reflect (emotionally). How do you feel as you read this passage?
- Interpret. What do you understand this passage to be saying? At this stage commentaries are important and helpful.
- Decision. What are you going to do in the light of your engagement with this passage?

Locally

If you want to explore more fully the importance of context for biblical teaching and learning, Louise Lawrence's excellent book *The Word in Place*[24] is very helpful. Louise explores in great depth contextual Bible study and teaching and the ways in which where we are affects how we engage with biblical teaching, and how biblical teaching forms us on the adventure of discipleship.

Do a review/audit of the biblical teaching in your community or church. How creative is it? Does it fully cater for a range of learning styles? In what ways does it lead to Kingdom action?

Globally

What global issues might your engagement with biblical teaching be calling you to get involved with? And what contemporary global issues might be sending you back to the Bible with questions and concerns?

Invite people of different nationalities and ethnicities to share how their cultures and situations impact how they engage with and live out biblical teaching. Then reflect on how their perspectives either complement or challenge your own.

Recognising the importance of biblical teaching for forming disciples you may wish to support an organisation that translates the Bible or provides Bibles in countries where access to the Bible is difficult.

A Biblical Passage to Reflect Upon
• 2 Timothy 3:16–17

What do you notice in this passage?

What will you do or change in the light of what you have read and noticed?

Recommended Reading
• Walter Brueggemann, *The Word That Redescribes the World*.
• Louise Lawrence, *The Word in Place*.
• Sue Wallace, *Multi-sensory Scripture*.

Endnotes
1. Norman Ivison, *expressions: making a difference*, Fresh Expressions, 2011, Ch 28. Or freshexpressions.org.uk/resources/makingadifference/28.

2. James D.G. Dunn, *The Acts of the Apostles*, Peterborough: Epworth, 1996, p35.

3. Santos Yao, 'Dismantling Social Barriers through Table Fellowship' in R.L. Gallagher and P. Hertig, *Mission in Acts*, New York: Orbis, 2004, p31.

4. Acts 2:14–36.

5. From Joel and the Psalms.

6. Sylvia Wilkey-Collinson, *Making Disciples*, Milton Keynes: Paternoster, 2004, p241.

7. This resonates strongly with the rhythm of being with Jesus and being sent out by him advocated by Steven Croft that we noted in Chapter 2.

8. 1 Corinthians 12:28.

9. Sylvia Wilkey-Collinson, *Making Disciples*, Milton Keynes: Paternoster, 2004, p241.

10. Loveday Alexander, *Acts: The People's Bible Commentary*, Oxford: Bible Reading Fellowship, 2006, p36.

11. biblesociety.org.uk/about-bible-society/our-work/lyfe/what-is-lyfe/.

12. godlyplay.uk.

13. messychurch.org.uk.

14. There are different approaches to this practice. For an alternative approach see

Ian Mobsby and Mark Berry, *A New Monastic Handbook*, Norwich: Canterbury Press, 2014, p91–92.

15. lindisfarne-scriptorium.co.uk.

16. If you are reading this in Essex, this was 1983. I'm sure Basildon is much nicer now.

17. Luke 6:46–49.

18. Walter Brueggemann, *The Word That Redescribes the World*, Minneapolis: Fortress Press, 2006, pxiv.

19. Ibid.

20. Psalm 119:105.

21. John 1:14.

22. John 20:30–31.

23. 2 Timothy 3:16.

24. Louise Lawrence, *The Word in Place*, London: SPCK, 2009.

9

Fellowship

They devoted themselves to the apostles' teaching and fellowship.
Acts 2:42

I have a theory that the amount we enjoy a wedding is often inversely proportionate to the amount of money spent on it. When I was minister of a church in Edlington, an ex-pit village near Doncaster, we had a particularly fabulous wedding. The bride came from a Tongan family so the day ran to Tongan timing. Vi duly arrived forty-five minutes late having practised the cultural tradition of saying goodbye to each room of the family home. The service began and was a joyous fusion of British and Tongan culture with hymns being sung simultaneously in two languages. Somehow, to my amazement, we all ended up at the end of 'O for a Thousand Tongues' at more or less the same time.

The wedding was produced on a very modest budget so the reception was held in the church hall which the small congregation had transformed into a beautifully decorated space. The bride's father had cooked all of the food in a massive oil drum in his front garden, building layers of meat, chicken and fish interspersed with potatoes which absorbed the flavours of the layers either side and tasted fabulous. No expense had been wasted on caterers so we, the guests, donned aprons, rolled up our sleeves and served the food, taking care to avoid getting meat juices all over our frocks and suits. And after the sumptuous banquet we piled back into the kitchen and did all the washing up before being inducted into the art of Tongan folk dancing. *Strictly Come Dancing* it wasn't, but it was a most wonderful day when the Spirit brought together different cultures, spoke through different languages, and through generous giving, practical action and prayer produced a sense of fellowship that was priceless and inspirational.

Koinonia

The Greek word translated as 'fellowship' in Acts 2 is *koinonia*. It is a word rich in depth, meaning and challenge. It points to a quality of relationship and activity which is so, so much deeper than the chit chat over a tepid cup of tea and a soggy digestive that sadly passes for fellowship in many places.

Koinonia is profoundly practical and deeply relational. John Stott argues that this *koinonia* 'is a Trinitarian experience, it is our common share in God, Father, Son and Holy Spirit. It also expresses what disciples of Jesus share together, what we give as well as what we receive.'[1]

C.K. Barrett suggests that the fellowship was 'based upon common acceptance of the apostolic message [and] came into action in charitable use of its material resources.'[2] Ben Witherington suggests that the term means 'a participation or sharing in common with someone else.'[3] David Watson points out that '*koinonia* in the New Testament occurs more frequently in the context of the sharing of money or possessions than in any other.'[4]

The *koinonia* in Acts 2 is seen in followers of Jesus eating, praying and sharing goods together. In short, sharing their lives with each other and the world around, in a prophetic symbol of the Kingdom of God. A powerful sign of a Spirit-filled way of life that stands against the sinfulness of selfishness. A wonder of hope, reconciliation and generosity. A true community of belonging and service.

The Rediscovery of Koinonia

Such fellowship was a powerful engine of mission and discipleship in the first century and remains so today. As we noted in Chapter 6, Roger Walton identifies intentional Christian community as one of the three primary formational energies for the adventure of discipleship.[5] Through the practical expression of Christ-like love *koinonia* draws people to Jesus and nurtures and sustains disciples as they follow. It is evangelistic (good news), pastoral, practical and formative.

Jean Vanier founded the L'Arche community 'to live out the Gospel and to follow Jesus Christ more closely'.[6] He did so to create a place of wholeness, belonging and fellowship for those with a range of abilities and disabilities, in particular those with significant mental health issues who felt 'excluded, worthless and unloved'. He says that:

> It is through everyday life *in community* and the love that must be incarnate in this, that people can discover that they have a value, that they are loved and so lovable.
>
> Each day brings me new lessons on how much Christian life must grow in commitment to life in community, and on how much that life needs faith, the love of Jesus and the presence of the Holy Spirit if it is to deepen.[7]

Vanier's vision of deep, committed, transformational community reflects the picture that Luke paints of the very first Christian communities which formed after the great outpouring of the Spirit.

An Urgent Need

In recent years there has been a rediscovery of the importance of authentic community for both presenting a vision of the Kingdom and for growing disciples. This rediscovery of the place of community, *koinonia*, true fellowship has not come a moment too soon. We live in a world that has never been more connected. At the click of button

I can Skype my friend Nick in Canada, email my friend Howard in Hong Kong or make a short film and send it to my sister in France via Twitter. Every day I get friend requests via Facebook and occasionally I am promised large sums of money if I send my bank account details to people who sound very friendly. And yet I live in Britain which, according to *The Independent*,[8] has been voted the loneliest country in Europe.

This epidemic of loneliness has been growing for many years. As far back as 1980 Jean Vanier noted that:

Contemporary society is the product of the disintegration of more or less natural or familial groupings. Towns are made up of neighbours who do not know each other – and this will soon be true of villages too. Human community is no longer found in the street, the neighbourhood or the village.

This state of things brings a loneliness which some people have difficulty in coping with.[9]

Claire Dalpa interviewed several fresh expressions about the fellowship they shared. She found that:

The communities . . . see the way they live together as the most valuable witness they can make in our individualist and anxiety-ridden society. They offer a counter-cultural lifestyle of hope and purpose to the lonely through living more intentionally in community.[10]

New monasticism in particular has helped to reconnect contemporary disciples of Jesus with the ancient practices of *koinonia*. One stream within new monasticism that has done this particularly well with younger people is the 24-7 Boiler Room Community[11] which has grown out of the 24-7 prayer movement. As intentional Christian communities Boiler Rooms are committed to a Rule of Life centred on three loves:

- *love for God* practised through prayer and creativity
- *love for one another* practised through hospitality and mercy

• *love for the world* practised through evangelism and learning

This Rule of Life is expressed through six practices or holy habits as the 24-7 website explains:[12]

1. Prayer and Worship: All Boiler Rooms seek to love God with a heartbeat of prayer and worship. Everything flows out from prayer and back into God's presence too. We value 'all kinds of prayers on all occasions' including adoration, petition, intercession, contemplation and spiritual warfare. Some Boiler Rooms are called to pray continually, night-and-day, while others pursue a rhythm of prayer through the week.

2. Creativity: All Boiler Rooms seek to love God by celebrating his creativity in all we do. We nurture generous imaginations and cultivate artistic expressions of prayer and worship through art, sculpture, cooking, music, poetry, dance, fun and a celebratory lifestyle.

3. Justice and Mercy: All Boiler Rooms seek to love people through lifestyles of justice and mercy, engaging with the needs of the poor, speaking up for the oppressed and fighting the structures of sin.

4. Hospitality: All Boiler Rooms seek to love people through hospitality, welcoming strangers into our lives and homes, sharing meals and nurturing friendships across boundaries of race and culture.

5. Evangelism: All Boiler Rooms seek to love the world by actively sharing the good news of Jesus with those who have not yet received him, through the incarnation and verbal proclamation.

6. Learning: All Boiler Rooms seek to love the world through training and discipleship, so that we continually grow in faith, in life, in wisdom and in effectiveness.

The type of fellowship that we read of in Acts 2 and that we see in communities such as Boiler Rooms and L'Arche offer a relational way of living that provides the love, togetherness and support that counteracts the forces of individualism and isolation. People need to be loved and real fellowship loves deeply.

Open and Welcoming

In their excellent book *Punk Monk*, Andy Freeman and Pete Greig point out that there are risks involved with seeking to form *koinonia*, community. Quoting Dietrich Bonhoeffer, who concluded that 'he who loves community destroys community' they go on to say:

> If community itself becomes our aim, we risk becoming elitist, considering that we are somehow more learned or authentic than others. If pursuing community itself becomes our aim, we lose the sense of welcome, lest the stranger unsettle our balance.[13]

This is a trap that so many Christian communities, newer and older, have fallen into. Self-identifying themselves as 'friendly' they have ceased to be welcoming. Those new to the community ironically feel excluded by the commitment that established members have to each other. Andy and Pete suggest the way to avoid following into the trap of excluding fellowship is to constantly centre the community on Jesus not the community itself. Jesus who calls and welcomes all sorts.

So we need to constantly work at welcome and openness. Hospitality is a big part of this and, as Chapter 14 will explore more fully, eating together can play a major part here. We also need to work hard at honesty. Truthfulness and integrity are vital in community. Part of this involves creating a climate in which it is not just OK but positively encouraged to ask questions and express doubts.

Then we need to strive to be attentive, to be generous with the time we offer to others and take genuine interest in other people, letting what is important to them become important to us. Christian psychologist Sara Savage puts it this way:

> To be listened to well is as close to the experience of being loved as to be barely indistinguishable.[14]

Take a little time to reflect on this. When have you felt most loved? For many of us it will be when we sensed someone had all the time in the world for us. When someone really listened, really cared. And when have you felt most unloved? Probably it was when you felt ignored, unwelcome, excluded.

Romantics Need Not Apply

There is a risk when exploring community, hospitality or *koinonia* that we do so via romantic lenses seeing an ideal world of tranquillity and harmony. The reality is often very different even in the positive stories told in this chapter. Fellowship needs working at. It needs working at practically. The *koinonia* of the early church didn't just happen. It emerged as the first followers of Jesus lived and worked together. One of the best places for fellowship to form is at the kitchen sink. As we serve by washing and drying so we talk and share stories and get to know each other.

Fellowship also needs working at relationally. In her brilliant book *I Am Somewhere Else*, Barbara Glasson reflects personally and theologically on being part of the emerging Bread Church in Liverpool. She celebrates all the good she experienced in and through the fellowship there but is also engagingly honest about the struggles in practising *koinonia*:

> We argue. We jostle for space, for attention, for praise. We want to be honoured, to be left alone, to be laughed with, to be special. We are defensive, we are possessive, we want to be inventive, we want to make bread, we do not want to mess up.[15]

As the writer of Ecclesiastes reminds us, 'there is nothing new under the sun'.[16] Barbara could easily have been describing the first intentional Christian community – the twelve that Jesus first called to follow.

It's not easy which is why God pours out his Spirit. The spirit that produces love, joy, peace, patience, kindness, generosity, faithfulness, gentleness and self-control.[17] The fruit that makes fellowship work, and that makes true fellowship a sign and wonder of Kingdom community.

Be Safe

When forming community it is of paramount importance that it is done safely. In any situation involving human relationships there is always a risk of abuse. Christian communities are not exempt from this so it is vital that Safeguarding policies specifically designed to create holistic Christian communities of holiness, love and care are developed and followed in any group living out the adventure of Christian discipleship.

Committed

In Chapter 7 we noted the little phrase that Luke uses to introduce his pen portrait of the nascent Christian community: 'they devoted themselves'. Characteristic of all intentional communities that develop deep and fruitful disciples is a high level of commitment to meeting together, using time well and living-out of love for God and those God calls them to serve.

I was blessed as a young person to grow up in a church community that valued younger people. Amongst many in the church who cared for us, loved us and put up with us in our formative years, were Alun and Rose. Their commitment was astonishing. Every Sunday evening they opened their home to us and when numbers grew so much that we couldn't fit in, they extended their home. We were welcomed, we were loved, we were listened to. We were served cakes that would put Mary Berry to shame (Rose was the most wonderful cook). We had our hearts repaired when teenage love fell apart. And we were encouraged in our discipleship; taken to evangelistic events where the call of Jesus was clearly presented, encouraged to join in with all sorts of acts of service in the community and given opportunities to explore particular calls and forms of ministry.

Alun and Rose's home was a place of true *koinonia*, of deep loving formative community.

A Foundational Habit

Like biblical teaching, fellowship is a foundational holy habit. As we have seen it has its challenges and complexities but as it takes root and grows it helps to create the space and build the relationships that allow the other habits to flourish.

Suggestions for Further Reflection and Action

Personally

The writer to the Hebrews urges us to not stop meeting together.[18] With whom are you meeting regularly in intentional fellowship? Who might you invite to join you? Do you need to be part of or form a new group?

With whom do you struggle to share fellowship? Pray for God's grace to bring renewal to any difficult relationships.

Locally

How fresh are the fellowship groups in your church? Is Christ the focus or have the groups become insular? Are newcomers really welcome? Do some new groups need to be formed?

Who are the lonely in your community? How could you form fellowship in a way that 'sets the lonely in families'[19] of Christian community?

Globally

Many forms of inspiring and fruitful intentional Christian communities have their origins in various countries around the world. The house churches of China. The Base Ecclesial Communities of Latin America. The Cell Churches of Korea. Take some time to learn from these.

For many followers of Jesus the only way to meet safely is in the privacy and secrecy of their homes. Pray for those for whom fellowship has to be lived in this way.

A Biblical Passage to Reflect On
• Romans 12:9–21

What do you notice in this passage?

What will you do or change in the light of what you have read and noticed?

Recommended Reading
•Barbara Glasson, *I Am Somewhere Else.*

- Ian Mobsby and Mark Berry, *A New Monastic Handbook.*
- Jean Vanier, *Community and Growth.*

Endnotes

1. John Stott, *The Message of Acts*, Leicester: Inter Varsity Press, 1990, p.83.

2. C.K. Barrett, *Acts 1–14 ICC*, Edinburgh: T&T Clark, 2004, p164.

3. Ben Wittherington, *The Acts of the Apostles: a Socio-Rhetorical Commentary*, Grand Rapids: Erdmans, 1988, p160.

4. David Watson, *Discipleship*, London: Hodder and Stoughton, 1981, p43.

5. Roger Walton, *Disciples Together*, London: SCM Press, 2014, p33.

6. Jean Vanier, *Community and Growth*, London: Darton, Longman and Todd, 198, p3.

7. Ibid.

8. http://www.independent.co.uk/life-style/health-and-families/features/the-loneliness-epidemic-more-connected-than-ever-but-feeling-more-alone-10143206.html.

9. Jean Vanier, *Community and Growth*, London: Darton, Longman and Todd, 198, p1.

10. Encounters on the Edge no. 38: *The Cost of Community: Issues of Maturity*, Sheffield: Church Army, 2008, p23.

11. 24-7prayer.com/communities.

12. 24-7prayer.com/communities/practices.

13. Andy Freeman and Pete Greig, *Punk Monk*, Eastbourne: Kingsway, 2007, p100.

14. Beta course.

15. Barbara Glasson, *I Am Somewhere Else*, London: Darton, Longman and Todd, 2006, p28.

16. Ecclesiastes 1:9.

17. Galatians 5:22–23.

18. Hebrews 10:25.

19. Psalm 68:6 NIV.

10
Breaking Bread

Day by day, as they spent much time together in the temple, they broke
bread at home.
Acts 2:46

One beautiful summer morning I gathered in the sunshine with a group[1] to break bread and share wine. The 'communion table' was a tree stump. The service we shared was simple, beautiful, holy. In the midst of God's first great act, creation, we celebrated his second great act, salvation. As the wine was offered to us it was done so with the words 'welcome to paradise'. This truly was a foretaste of the heavenly banquet. Such was its beauty and holiness I found myself having to sit down transfixed and transformed by the majesty of the occasion.

In conversation about the breaking of bread, or Holy Communion, one prominent Christian leader, who I value as a friend, asked, 'Why have we made something Jesus deliberately made so simple and transferable, so complicated?' It is a good question that she asks.

In the Beginning

In Acts the emerging church is regulation light (no mention is made of the apostles presiding at the breaking of bread) and blessed with nimbleness conducive to growth. There is much to learn from this. Also noteworthy is the context. 'They broke bread at home,' says Luke. Note the distinction between temple and home in verse 46 of Acts 2. And of course the Lord's Supper was inaugurated and first celebrated in the upper room of a home by Jesus who was born in Bethlehem – which intriguingly means 'house of bread'. The discipleship meal began in an everyday, domestic context. Sacred in its simplicity. Transferable and transcultural. Accessible to all.

The breaking of bread is a term that Luke uses elsewhere, most powerfully in Luke 24:35 when Cleopas and his companion describe how Jesus had been made known to them 'in the breaking of the bread'. It is not clear from the text of Acts 2:42 how Luke is using the term when describing the life of the first Christian communities and the commentators are cagey about its use. Is it describing the act which opened a common Jewish meal? Is it a specific sacramental act? C.K. Barrett argues that 'the "breaking of bread" was not a Jewish term for a meal and in this sense must have been a Christian development'[2] i.e. an embryonic service of Holy Communion. James Dunn is more circumspect suggesting that 'We may assume that on some occasions at least the meal included a shared commemoration of the Last Supper but Luke has not gone out of his way to make this plain'.[3]

Could Luke be fusing together both meanings and usages? Does Acts 2:42 remind us that, at heart, the Lord's Supper is actually very simple and very flexible? An everyday event infused with sacred significance. A holy habit to be practised with due reverence for the one who instituted it, anytime, anyplace, anywhere. Whenever believers meet together they can break bread as part of a meal as well as part of an act of worship, and not just remember but experience the risen Jesus in the midst of their *koinonia*. Hans Conzelmann points out that Luke makes no attempt to distinguish between an ordinary meal and the 'Eucharist' and suggests that 'the unity of the two is part of the ideal picture of the earliest church'.[4] The unity of the two is seen particularly powerfully in the Eucharistic meal that Paul shared with his fellow sailors in Acts 27:35. Their meal on the ship began with Paul giving thanks and breaking bread. Encouraged and renewed spiritually they were then nourished and strengthened physically as they ate together.

In this chapter I have used the term 'breaking of bread' in an open way consistent with Luke's usage as understood by Conzelmann and others. So sometimes the term is used to represent a simple sharing of bread and sometimes it is used in reference to a Eucharistic act of worship. As you read on you may wish to interpret the term and my usage of it through the tradition that you are part of.

A family meal

The domestic context in which the breaking of bread began as a holy habit of Christian discipleship also supports the view that it is a practice that should be partaken of by children. This view is reinforced by the active presence of Jewish children at the Passover Meal, the celebration of creation and salvation, at a sharing of which Jesus instituted what became the Lord's Supper.

Much is made of the majesty and mystery of Holy Communion and rightly so. In my experience it is many of the children with whom I have broken bread and shared wine who, with eyes wide open in wonder, have entered most deeply into the holiness and transcendence of the sacrament. And just as the questions of the Jewish children at a Passover meal help the adults deepen their understanding of the significance of the meal they share, so, too, do the honest questions of children exploring the meaning of the Lord's Supper.

Anytime, Anyplace, Anywhere

The breaking of bread is a worshipful, pastoral and a missional act, and one that can be shared in any context.

Jesus introduced the practice of breaking bread in the context of worship characterised by thanksgiving.[5]

The Lord Jesus on the night when he was betrayed took a loaf of bread, and when he had given thanks . . .[6]

For many disciples of Jesus, from a range of traditions, the breaking of bread is the high point of worship, celebrating God's loving acts in creation and salvation.

I have broken bread in homes, cafés, beside hospital beds and in prison. Pastorally it nourishes the soul, deepens devotion, renews, transforms, refreshes, heals and humbles. It reminds us of the sacrificial nature of discipleship, following the one who gave himself sacrificially out of love for all. It also unites. When we stretch out our hands to receive the bread and the cup we are all the same – sinners being transformed by grace. It has been my privilege to place bread into the hands of scrap dealers and bishops. Hands contorted with arthritis and the smooth-skinned hands of children. The hands of those who I find it easy to love and the hands of those I struggle to love. Black hands, white hands, eager hands and hesitant hands. All being touched and transformed by grace as they take hold of the bread of life.

On the adventure of discipleship the breaking of bread is also being shared in all sorts of creative missional ways to make God's love known. As one church report puts it:

The nourishment we receive is not for ourselves alone, but in order that God may empower us to go out into the world, find out what God is doing there and join in.[7]

Father Michael Clarke is an Anglican priest in Barbados. One Palm Sunday morning he arrived at his church and told his startled young curate to take care of the service whilst he took a table to celebrate and share the Eucharist at the roadside. Cars stopped, those walking came over and there amidst the bustle of journeys and business the body and blood of Christ were shared.

My friend and former President of the Methodist Church Inderjit Bhogal tells the wonderful story of an occasion when he broke bread on a park bench.

Albert is homeless. He says people call him a 'tramp' and sometimes give him money. He lives on the streets of Sheffield where I have got to know him well. As a walker, he gave me sound advice as I prepared to walk along roads from Sheffield to London. I saw him recently, he was sitting on a concrete bench in the city centre. He had a bandage round his head and one round his foot. 'Banged into a wall,' he said.

As we got into conversation, I asked him to help me. 'I'm working on a sermon about tables and bread and parties in the wilderness,' I said, 'it seems a bit odd but can you help me?'

'I love bread,' he said.

He reached into a carrier bag beside him. His boots and walking stick were by the bag. Out of the bag he fetched bread.

'I always have bread,' he said. 'I know a shop. I turn up just before closing time. They give me a couple of loaves. With it I feed myself and my brothers and sisters who are poor.' He talked to me about all those homeless ones who walk at night as others sleep.

He held out a large round cob.

'This is made from rye. I love it – my favourite,' he said, 'try some.'

He broke off a large piece with his rugged hands and held it out to me. I received it and said 'Amen' and ate it in bits over several minutes.

As I ate it, he unpacked his carrier bag and brought out different kinds of bread and placed it all on the concrete slab bench which had now become a table. Suddenly I was having a meal, and he was the host. Each loaf was held up and its contents were described. I was given a piece from each loaf.

'You need good red wine with this bread . . . it would be a good one for your communion at church.'

'You need to eat this bread with cheese . . .'

All around us a city centre environment with its own beauty, but a wilderness with a lifestyle of grabbing and greed and of profit before people. People racing about. Some sitting down to rest. Before me now a parable of the text: 'a table in the wilderness.'

I was being fed by one of the poorest people I know. I was a guest of honour at a table in the wilderness. 'You treat me like an honoured guest.'[8]

A Gift to Share

A growing number of 'Bread Churches' have the baking and breaking of bread at the heart of their shared life. A key part of the life of many Bread Churches is the giving away of much of the bread they make. A simple act of kindness. A symbolic sign of selfishness being overcome and generosity prevailing. A prophetic act of witness in an often acquisitive and greedy world. An act of solidarity with the materially poorest. A simple living-out of Jesus' call to feed the hungry. A symbol of God's generosity and the Kingdom that is so often depicted as a banquet.

Somewhere Else in Liverpool, started by Barbara Glasson, was an early example of a Bread Church. Writing about their practice of giving bread away she said:

Making bread and giving it away is a personable activity. It is also subversive. In a capitalist economy that relies on trade, giving something as essential as bread as a gift is counter-cultural.[9]

When sharing bread we do need to remember that around 1 per cent of people have coeliac disease and therefore need gluten-free bread. We need to take care when we share this holy habit which is meant to be inclusive that we don't inadvertently exclude people.

A Converting Ordinance

John Wesley (who practised the holy habit of breaking bread on a daily basis) believed that Holy Communion was 'a converting ordinance'. A few years ago I spoke with a number of leaders of newly forming Christian communities – fresh expressions of church – about the part Holy Communion played in forming and nurturing disciples of Jesus. Andy Jones at Grace Church Hackney said:

We've seen Holy Communion act as a barometer of discipleship and as a spur to discipleship. We've seen a number of people move through the stages of watching, praying, coming forward but not partaking until they finally reach a stage of eating and drinking in faith. Similarly we've noticed some stop eating and this has given us discipleship openings and opportunities.

Meanwhile Ben Edson who was then leading Sanctus 1 in Manchester told me:

Communion is central to Sanctus 1. It is the way that people feel part of the community, and for some has been a rite of passage into the community. It helps sustain community and focus us on the central focus of our discipleship – the person of Christ.

Simple and Transferable

Why have we made something Jesus deliberately made so simple and transferable so complicated? The question remains but happily, as we have seen, there are those who are thinking imaginatively and creatively; pastorally and missionally.

In Shropshire a group of churches were concerned for those in their communities who were housebound, some of whom used to attend church services but were no longer able to. So they set aside a lady called Trish to break bread as part of an extended communion in the homes of several housebound people. What began as a pastoral exercise with small groups of Christian disciples practising holy habits together, soon became a missional enterprise with the homes becoming hope-filled holy habitats, as those blessed by Trish and the habit of breaking bread invited their neighbours to join with them. Small missional communities forming around the holy habit of breaking bread.

Sacramental

The breaking of bread is truly sacramental – i.e. an outward sign of an invisible grace, a sacred symbol of God's life-giving love. As we practise the holy habit of breaking bread it becomes so much more than a simple shared meal. What we see, sense and experience in the breaking of bread we begin to see, sense and experience elsewhere; everywhere even. We become alive to creation and salvation, we see, sense and experience signs of God's love all around. And, as Barbara Glasson suggests, we become what we share, and what we share represents what we are: a blessed, broken, thankful and shared people.

Suggestions for Further Reflection and Action

Personally

Ponder the question of why have we made something Jesus deliberately made so simple and transferable so complicated.

In what ways could the breaking of bread be a holy habit for you in your everyday life?

With whom could you share a simple act of breaking bread? Your family? A housebound neighbour perhaps? Or the person at work who always seems to eat their lunch on their own? Let the sacred be present in the everyday.

Locally

Does your church make provision for those who are gluten intolerant? And when sharing wine as well, does your church make provision for those who cannot drink alcohol?

Pray through ways in which you could be adventurous in practising this holy habit:

- Could you celebrate the breaking of bread outside, in the park or by the roadside?
- Could your church develop a bread making and sharing ministry? For more on this visit hobstafford.co.uk/bread-church or somewhere-else.org.uk
- Could you plant small missional communities that gather around the holy habit of breaking bread?

Globally

Explore how bread is broken and shared in different countries around the world. What does this teach us about the essence of this sacramental act?

Partner with a Christian community in another country that is seeking to live out its life as a blessed, broken, thankful and shared people. See what you can receive as gift from them and what you can give as gift to them.

A Biblical Passage to Reflect On

• 1 Corinthians 11:23–26

What do you notice in this passage?

What will you do or change in the light of what you have read and noticed?

Recommended Reading

• Barbara Glasson, *Mixed-up Blessing.*

• Mary Gray-Reeves and Michael Perham, *The Hospitality of God.*

• The Methodist Church, *His Presence Makes the Feast.*

Endnotes

1. This was at a Beloved Life retreat led by Ian and Gail Adams www.belovedlife. org.

2. C.K. Barrett, *Acts 1–14, ICC,* Edinburgh: T&T Clark, 2004, p165.

3. James D.G. Dunn, *The Acts of the Apostles,* Peterborough: Epworth, 1996, p35.

4. Hans Conzelmann, *The Acts of the Apostles,* Philadelphia: Fortress, 1987, p23.

5. The term Eucharist that many traditions use to denote the sacramental practice of breaking bread comes from the Greek verb *eucharisto,* meaning 'to give thanks'.

6. 1 Corinthians 11:23–24.

7. *Share this feast:* The Methodist Church, 2006, p38.

8. Inderjit Bhogal, *A Table For All: A Challenge to Church and Nation.* Penistone: Penistone Publications, 2000.

9. Barbara Glasson, *Mixed-up Blessing,* Peterborough: Inspire, 2006, p50.

11
Prayer

They devoted themselves to the apostles' teaching and fellowship, to the breaking of bread and the prayers.
Acts 2:42

Every now and then, when I invite a group to pray I will say, 'Let us pray,' pause for a moment and then ask people to open their eyes and reflect upon what they have done. Most, if not all, on hearing the words 'let us pray' close their eyes, put their hands together and slightly bow their heads. And there is nothing wrong with that. I do it myself very often. The posture expresses devotion, and the hands and closed eyes say this is important and I want to concentrate on this. All good stuff. But there is so much more to prayer than this and so many ways in which we can experience and live the most frequently practised of the holy habits.

The Breath of God – The Breath of Life
At a Beloved Life retreat, Gail Adams explained to those of us gathered there that the Hebrew name of God, Yahweh, not only has no vowels

151

(so should be spelt Yhwh) but actually can be expressed without using the tongue or vocal chords by the sound of our breathing in and breathing out.

In the second creation story of Genesis 2[1] God breathes life into humankind. In the New Testament one of the Greek words for the Spirit is *pneuma* meaning 'air' or 'breath'. In John's Gospel the risen Jesus breathes on the disciples so that they may receive the Holy Spirit.[2]

True prayer is so much more than something we do occasionally or regularly. Prayer is the spiritual air we breathe. We breathe in the grace, blessings, peace, courage, holiness of God and breathe out our adoration, praise, thanksgiving, confession and intercession.

Prayer is an adventure in itself. In prayer we soar and struggle, wonder and worry. When we pray we can experience ecstasy and anguish, clarity and confusion. We encounter mystery and silence. When we run out of words the Spirit breathes out and prays through our groans and sighs.[3]

Luke Loved Prayer

Prayer is one of the major themes of both Luke's Gospel and Acts. It is no surprise to see Luke presenting prayer as one of the hallmarks of the first Christian communities. In the immediate aftermath of the Pentecost events the focus is on spontaneous, unstructured prayer in either native or unlearned languages (or tongues).[4] The disciples are on fire. The praying is spontaneous, passionate, energetic and noisy. Prayer is celebratory, visionary, confident and expectant. Such times of prayer are a gift to be treasured.

When I was a student in York I served as President of the university Christian Union. One evening we met as a leadership team with the leaders of many of the churches from across the city. We met in an upper room and began to pray. As we prayed I experienced a real Pentecost moment. The room was so full of energy it seemed to be shaking. It was really noisy, too. I opened my eyes at one point to check that the room wasn't falling apart. I suddenly felt a great warmth going through my body – as if I had drunk a big glass of red wine in one go (I hadn't, just in case you're worried). The Holy Spirit filled us in that moment in a way that I had never known before. Sometimes prayer can be like that.

Sometimes, often, usually, it is much more routine. By the time we get to Acts 2:42 Luke slips in the little phrase *the prayers.* The use of the plural with the definite article implies the use of certain specific, regularly used prayers. The church of Jesus began as a movement within what the scholars call Second Temple Judaism so the shared prayers of the communities described in Acts would have been mainly Jewish prayers with added Christian flavouring. F.F. Bruce suggests that the 'community's prayers would follow Jewish models, but their content would be enriched because of the Christ event'.[5]

C.K. Barrett follows a similar line to F.F. Bruce suggesting that the Lord's Prayer may have been included[6] in the formal prayers of the community (not unreasonable in the light of Luke 11:2-4 which includes the instruction, 'When you pray, say'). He goes on to suggest that in Acts 2:42-47, Luke was describing Christian activities not only from the immediate aftermath of the outpouring of the Spirit at Pentecost but also from his own time and place later on in the life of the nascent Christian community.[7]

So very early on in the Christian tradition we have spontaneous and set prayers both playing a valuable part in living the adventure of discipleship. Similarly public and private prayer. A reminder to us not to be too precious about our preferred ways of praying.

Who We Are is How We Pray

Whilst we should not be too precious about the ways we find it most helpful to pray, there is nothing wrong with courteously naming and sharing our preferences. I have prayed in all sorts of ways and have friends whose preferred forms of prayer vary widely. So I have charismatic friends who pray exuberantly in their native language and other tongues, and contemplative friends who like to breathe their prayers in and out in silence. I have friends who pray with their bodies as well as their words and friends who use symbols, candles and icons as part of their praying. I have friends with special needs who pray in a language all of their own, whose joy in praying is clear on their faces. Other friends like to write, read, paint or dance their prayers. My friend Jemima has recently started leading prayer and pilates classes.

Diversity is a good thing. God has coloured it into creation and blessed humanity with a range of personality types. In his intriguing book *Who We Are is How We Pray* Charles Keating explores how our personality types affect the ways in which we prefer to pray. He, too, affirms the value of diversity:

> Sometimes we still assume that the human part of us needs to be subjugated if we are to become holy [but] to suppress our created humanity is to set God against himself. He who created the human said it was good. The God of creation is the God of grace. It is interesting that within the theory of Myers-Briggs there are no bad personalities; there are only different personalities. And different personalities need different spiritualties.[8]

God-centred Prayer

In understanding our preferences in prayer and delighting in the many different ways in which we can pray it is important to not lose sight of the divine community which is the source, focus and means by which we pray. When it comes to prayer it is so easy to rush to the request list and associate prayer with asking God for things or doing divine deals.

Prayer in all its fullness and richness re-orientates and establishes us in right relationships with God, those we love and the world God cares for. It is a holy and transformative habit and way of being. It is also an antidote to the selfishness that is sin.

Adoration is an oft-neglected aspect of prayer. When did you last spend time expressing your adoration of God just for the sake of it? Reorienting yourself in the orbit of God's love. Gazing upon and being transformed by divine holiness.

Confession, too, can also be trivialised or, more seriously, rushed. Re trivialisation: I do wonder sometimes if God is less worried about us saying the odd rude word or drooling slightly too long over the latest self-publicity photo of a celebrity and more bothered about our attitudes to those who will drown today in the Mediterranean or die of preventable diseases. Regarding rushing this aspect of prayer: I worry that when it comes to confession that we (individually and especially collectively) are sometimes keen to get on with the repentance (the changing) without first dwelling in the place of contrition and sorrow.

Thanksgiving is another aspect of prayer to savour and be transformed by. Another part of prayer that fosters humility and the holy habit of gladness and generosity that we will explore in Chapter 14. The simple practice of saying grace before a meal connects us with the goodness of God in creation whilst the great Eucharistic prayers used in services of Holy Communion remind us of how much we have to be grateful for, most especially in the self-giving love of God seen in the life, death and resurrection of Jesus.

As we take time with adoration, confession and thanksgiving we are re-orientated to, and transformed by, the love and holiness of God. So when we come to intercession we will be able to pray in a way consistent with the teaching of Jesus for the fruits of God's Kingdom to be seen and known in the lives of those for whom we pray.

Prayer Transcending Boundaries

We noted earlier how spontaneous and repeated prayers are both important ways of praying that go right back to the beginnings of the Jesus movement. Commenting on Acts 2 Ernst Haenchen adds a further factor into the mix. He suggests that the first followers of Jesus may have had distinct times for Christian and Jewish prayers.

The prayers [referred to in Acts 2:42] are above all those offered together with the Jewish congregation. This by no means precludes the possibility that the Christians also had their own prayers and set times of devotion.[9]

If Haenchen is right then this presents an interesting opportunity and challenge in our multi-faith age. Can we/is it right to pray with or alongside those of other faiths?

> I was once travelling with a colleague along the A38 – a busy dual carriage way in Staffordshire. We were doing about 65 mph when we were clipped by a following vehicle spearing us into the barriers in the middle of the road which in turn pitched us into a roll. We came to a stop upside down in the middle of the road. Miraculously none of the following traffic hit us.
>
> We were trapped in the car. The first two people to come to our aid were two young Muslim men. They got me out of the car and mercifully I had just a few cuts and bruises. My friend, who had been driving and therefore not able to protect herself, was in a far worse state with a badly gashed head and a broken neck. When the paramedics very carefully extricated her from the car she asked if I would pray for her. So kneeling in the broken glass and blood I did. And as I prayed in the name of Jesus, the two young Muslims stood respectfully by, their heads bowed.
>
> Thankfully my friend went on to make a full recovery. I would not recommend rolling over on a busy road but I learnt a lot that day, not least about the respect those of other faiths have for us when we pray in the name of Jesus.

Much of this chapter deals with praying personally or as part of Christian gatherings. In the book of Acts prayer is not confined to the homes of believers or the temple. There is praying on the streets and in public places too. As the A38 story shows there are times when prayer in public is appropriate and indeed vital. Many followers of Jesus are taking steps of faith in praying in public through ventures such as healing on the streets.

> In Chapter 7 I owned up to being an Aston Villa fan. The parish church of St Peter and St Paul is located right next to Villa Park. On

match days a group of people from the church offer prayer for fans going to the match. One day I was hobbling along with a swollen knee that I had injured skiing. I'm going to have some prayer today, I thought to myself, slightly nervous of the comments that could have been forthcoming from passing fans. But as I sat there were no cheeky or rude comments just warm words of prayer from a couple of people from the church. After being prayed for I went on my way still hobbling, maybe a bit less so, feeling peaceful inside and grateful to those willing to bear witness to God's love on the streets. And, yes of course, Villa did lose.

In light of the need to be alert to growing sensitivities about how and where we can bear witness and pray, do take care to check what is appropriate and permissible in any public place where you might like to pray, particularly a place of work. And always ask for the permission of the person you feel led to pray for.

The Adventure of Prayer

Prayer, like discipleship, is an adventure. Sometimes as we pray, the Spirit surprises us.

Barbara Glasson spent a year walking the streets of Liverpool and listening before she did anything else, seeking to discern needs and how to form a new Christian community for the city. Then one day 'a word came straight into my head. The word was bread'.[10] For someone who was unused to 'God answering prayers directly'[11] and whose theological framework did not major on this sort of spiritual encounter, this was a startling but crucial moment.

Sometimes we do have to get out of the way and let God be God! We need to go with the flow and connect with the creativity of the Divine Community of Father, Son and Holy Spirit.

Refreshing Prayer

Of all the holy habits, prayer is the one most at risk of becoming dry and difficult. Over the centuries many of the great saints and heroes of the faith have shared honestly about the struggles they have had in prayer. St John of the Cross' famous poem *Dark Night of the Soul* explores the struggles we can endure as we seek to grow in spiritual maturity and union with God. In his sermon *The Wilderness State* John Wesley deals candidly with the times of dryness we experience along the way on the adventure of discipleship.

Dryness can have many causes. Sometimes we may just be physically exhausted and need a good rest or change of scene. At other times our selfishness (sin) may be marring our relationships with God and others and withering our prayer life. In which case we need to seek forgiveness through confession, contrition and repentance. Dryness can also be the result of tiredness with the way we have been praying. In which case trying something new and being creative can be really helpful. If you normally sit to pray why not go for a prayer walk or practise some 'body prayers'? If words are becoming stale why not draw or paint or sculpt? If you are normally very quiet when you pray why not find a suitable space and shout out your praise, your angst or your intercessions. Conversely if you are becoming a bit tired of shouting out your prayers why not sit still with a candle or icon and see where the Spirit takes you in prayer?

A note here to those who lead others in prayer. Just as variety is important to the development of a healthy individual prayer life, so, too, it is vital for fruitful gatherings of prayer. Sadly, too many prayer meetings become dry and predictable and we can guess who will pray and what they will pray about. Variety in prayer not only taps into the creativity of God but engages and inspires a greater range of prayers from those gathered.

There is an absolute wealth of resources available to help us with creative and different ways of praying. Books, websites, DVDs, conferences, retreats. I have listed some of the ones I would recommend at the end of this chapter. If none of these float your boat just ask around to see what others have found helpful.

When it comes to practising the habit of prayer there are so many ways of exploring and enjoying this life-giving, God-breathed gift.

Suggestions for Further Reflection and Action

Personally
Review the balance of your prayer life. Is it all a shopping list of requests or is there a healthy balance of adoration, confession, thanksgiving and intercession?

Have you refreshed the ways in which you pray recently? Try out some different ways of praying, maybe using some of the resources suggested below.

Locally
If you are part of a small group or a prayer meeting have an honest conversation about the ways of prayer that you find most helpful and most challenging.

Have a look at Charles Keating's book and consider how inclusive your prayer meetings or times of prayer are for a range of personality types.

If there is not a gathering for prayer in your community why not start one that is creative, adventurous and outward looking.

Globally
Pray for those who cannot gather publicly for prayer. What does their faithfulness teach us?

Buy a book of prayers from around the world and let the prayers of different cultures and countries enrich and inform your prayer life.

A Biblical Passage to Reflect On
• Luke 11:1–13

What do you notice in this passage?

What will you do or change in the light of what you have read and noticed?

Recommended Reading
• Pete Greig, *God on Mute*.

- Charles J. Keating, *Who We Are is How We Pray*.
- Sue Wallace, *Multi-sensory Prayer*.

Other Helpful Resources

Prayer websites
- belovedlife.org/author/ian-adams for Morning Bell prayers
- christianaid.org.uk/resources/churches/prayer/current-issues
- contemplativefire.org
- freshexpressions.org.uk/guide/worship
- pray-as-you-go.org
- prayingincolor.com

DVDs
- *Sacred Posture:* body prayers ancient and contemporary, choreographed by Philip Roderick.

Retreats/Conferences
- belovedlife.org

Creative Resources
- Messy Church resources: messychurch.org.uk
- Lindisfarne Scriptorium resources: lindisfarne-scriptorium.co.uk

Endnotes
1. Genesis 2:7.
2. John 20:22.
3. Romans 8:26.
4. Acts 2:4.
5. F.F. Bruce, *The Book of the Acts Revised*, Grand Rapids: Erdmans, 1988, p73.
6. C.K. Barrett, *Acts 1–14, ICC*, Edinburgh: T&T Clark, 2004, p166.
7. Ibid, p160.
8. Charles J. Keating, *Who We Are is How We Pray*, Mystic: Twenty-Third Publications, 2004, p3.
9. Ernst Haenchen, *The Acts of the Apostles*, Oxford: Basil Blackwell, 1971, p191.
10. Barbara Glasson, *Mixed-up Blessing*, Peterborough: Inspire, 2006, p3.
11. Ibid.

12
Giving

All who believed were together and had all things in common; they would sell their possessions and goods and distribute the proceeds to all, as any had need.
Acts 2:44–45

I was once at a meeting in Edinburgh as ferocious winds swept across Scotland. Tree roots were visibly lifting in the ground. It was like a scene from *Doctor Who*. When the meeting ended I went to Waverley Station to catch my train home only to find the station closed and all trains cancelled because of the weather. I needed to get back for some important meetings the next day so my friends John and Olive – who had already been very generous by hosting me in their home near Glasgow the night before – offered to drive me all the way to Carlisle (100 miles away) from where it was hoped trains would run that evening. I had a need, they had a car which they willingly, kindly and generously used to help get me home. I made it home shortly before midnight, not that long after John and Olive who had got stuck in the big traffic jam on the

M6 caused by all the extra people driving.

The Community of Goods

In Acts 2:44–45 and Acts 4:32–37 Luke presents pictures of the early Christian communities of disciples supporting one another and those in need in the wider community by the generous giving of their resources. They shared and sold possessions to create a common fund which could be used to support those in need of income or resources. The fund may also have supported the apostles and later on the deacons[1] and others set apart for ministries of preaching and service.

Such commitment was not unique to the first church. The Jewish Essene community based at Qumran near the north-west corner of the Dead Sea was centred on the teachings of *Torah* (the books of the law in the Hebrew Scriptures) and the obligatory sharing of possessions. According to the Jewish historian Josephus, the Essenes were noted for their sharing of possessions. 'Riches they despise, and their community of goods is truly admirable.'[2]

In contrast to the practice of the Essenes, the imperfect verb tense used in Acts 2:45 suggests that the selling of goods in the first Christian communities was not a one-off occurrence upon entry into the community but rather a recurrent practice, as and when need arose. F.F. Bruce sees in these verses echoes of the common purse that Jesus shared with his disciples.[3] James Dunn sees more evidence of spontaneity and 'eschatological enthusiasm'.[4]

A Fleeting Habit?

John Drane in his magisterial tome *Introducing the New Testament*[5] suggests that the type of giving described by Luke in the early chapters of Acts may not have lasted that long. Like James Dunn, John sees as distinctive the spontaneity of the giving of the first Christians. He too draws the contrast with Qumran where the sharing of resources was carefully regulated by various rules. He points out that the type of sharing described by Luke does not appear again in the New Testament after Acts 4 suggesting that 'the Christians ran out of money'.[6] He also points out that:

> The passages themselves make it clear that the members of the Jerusalem church did not dispose of everything at once but sold things as the need arose and then shared the profits with the rest of the Christian community.[7]

So it is also possible that this simply became the way things were done and Luke didn't feel the need to mention it again.

As we noted in Chapter 2, when looking at the call narratives, we need to be careful of suggestions that the first followers of Jesus gave away all of their resources in order to live 'by faith'. The evidence suggests they didn't but maintained businesses and other sources of income that sustained them and supported Jesus in his mission. There is nothing intrinsically wrong with earning a reasonable salary or running a profitable business. They can be and are valuable sources of regular and sustainable support for Christian mission.

Likewise the ownership of property. The role of the house church was critical in the spread of the gospel. The church grew by spreading from house to house. New communities could be established very quickly in villages, towns and cities. Bradley Blue argues that Acts provides a 'consistent pattern of the conversion of individuals who are capable of significant benefaction including houses in which the community gathered'.[8] He goes on to argue that:

> Consistently Paul's objective is the conversion of a home owner who is capable of benefaction, including a house which was used as the alternate venue in which the Christians assembled.[9], [10]

I'm not convinced the early Christians ran out of money or had no economic strategy. In my view it is more likely that the fervour that facilitated extravagant spontaneity cooled and sustainable systems of resourcing began to be developed.

The Giving of God

I have the dubious distinction of having degrees in economics and theology. The basic question addressed by economics is how we choose to use limited resources. As a follower of Jesus I want my theology to shape my economics – to inform and guide the decisions I make about resources. Both those I have been entrusted with and the resources belonging to the communities and organisations that I am part of.

The start point for any theological thinking is the nature of God. Giving is a key part of this nature and it is possible to read the Bible as a narrative of giving. In Genesis we see God gifting creation to humanity[11] to take care of and to enjoy. It is not long before selfishness (sin) damages both the gift and the relationships that were designed to let life flourish. But this does not stop God giving. Resources continue to be given both through the mundane and the miraculous. Wisdom, teaching and prophecy are given to guide and facilitate holy living. And then in the climactic words of John's Gospel:

God so loved the world that he gave his only Son, so that everyone who believes in him may not perish but may have eternal life.[12]

Even when this gift is rejected God keeps on giving. Giving new life to Jesus who had been crucified by the selfishness of sin. And then giving the gift of the Spirit at Pentecost that birthed the community that in turn was noted for its giving.

So when it comes to thinking about the holy habit of giving we need to start by locating that thinking within the generous, extravagant even, persistent giving of God.

Models of Giving

For many disciples today the practices of tithes and offerings as outlined in the Hebrew Scriptures[13] continue to inform and guide their giving of resources. This is common practice in many of the evangelical, pentecostal and charismatic churches that are growing in the UK today. There is no doubt these practices can and do release resources that are conducive to the growth and mission of Christian communities.

> Near where I live a new church was planted in the hall of a school. Within two years a community of around thirty were meeting regularly and had employed their own pastor. Some other local Christians looked on in a mix of awe, wonder and envy. 'How can you do that?' they asked. 'Because we tithe,' came the polite and succinct answer.

At this point it is important to note that whilst the practice of tithing is not rescinded in the New Testament it is not specifically endorsed by Jesus, Paul or anyone else either. This may be, of course, because it was simply accepted as a given – a continuation of Jewish practices.

Jesus talks about money more than any other subject but he never does so in a legalistic, percentage-based, prescriptive way. Rather he uses stories and examples to point people to the divine impulse of generous giving. For me the most moving and challenging story about giving is that often called the Widow's Mite.

> *[Jesus] looked up and saw rich people putting their gifts into the treasury; he also saw a poor widow put in two small copper coins. He said, 'Truly I tell you, this poor widow has put in more than all of them; for all of them have contributed out of their abundance, but she out of her poverty has put in all she had to live on.'*[14]

The sacrificial generosity of the widow is stunning but by no means unique. So often it is those who have the least financially or materially who are most generous with their giving. Simon Guillebaud tells a story that has been told by many receiving hospitality in homes of families that are materially poor but spiritually rich.

> I've been overwhelmed by the sacrificial sharing of destitute believers in Burundi. I drove to a displacement camp. They had no electricity, water or sanitation. After the church service, I was taken to a tin

shack, and fed beans and rice. I knew this was far beyond what they could afford. They were giving me so much out of their little, as so often we give so little out of so much.[15]

There are no percentages, rules or prescriptions here just extravagant generosity of Kingdom proportions.

Inspirational Generosity

The generous giving of Jesus inspired giving in others. Zacchaeus[16] knew a thing or two about percentages. As a tax collector he would have had formulas coming out of his ears. Overwhelmed by the gifts of salvation and affirmation from Jesus he gives not a tenth, not even a tenth and a bit more, but half of his possessions plus the offer to pay anyone he has defrauded four times what he greedily took from them. The economics of forgiveness are extraordinary!

As we note elsewhere, giving is a habit best practised in partnership with other holy habits. In particular with gladness and generosity. We give in response to the generosity of God and giving at its best is about offering the best we can in return. As Proverbs reminds us, giving should be a first thought, a first act, not a reluctant afterthought or begrudged gesture.

> Honour the LORD with your substance and with the first fruits of all your produce.[17]

The same is true of our giving to others. One of my school teachers, David Waller, once memorably explained the difference between an offering and a collection. An offering, he said, is what you give to your guests when they come round for a meal. A collection is what you gather up and give to the dog afterwards.

Forms of Giving

Giving is expressed in many forms. Obviously giving can be financial. It can involve the selling or sharing of goods and possessions which was such a hallmark of the first Christian communities described by Luke in Acts.

On the Fresh Expressions website Jennie Appleby shares some challenging thoughts from her time serving in a small northern town where she deliberately chose to live in an area that no estate agent would dare call 'desirable'. She says:

Life amongst this new community was transformative and there was never a dull moment. Frequent sights of furniture being moved between houses (usually on foot), early morning police raids and unconventional offers of cheap, electrical items were everyday occurrences. I realised I'd been accepted in the community when I was invited by two women to join them for a drink at the local working men's club, and when someone turned up on my doorstep to ask for prayer.

Amidst the colourful lives on the estate and the disbelief of Christians from the other side of town, I discovered a sense of the tangible presence of God. I could imagine Jesus himself walking the streets with me and I experienced signs of God's Kingdom: people sharing their lives and possessions together – not out of a sense of Christian love or duty but because they had so little themselves. I had never witnessed people sharing on this level before – they were teaching me lessons about how to live the Christian life.[18]

In societies that are experienced as cash rich but time poor the gift of time has a particular value. Here Jesus offers a perfect example, giving time to children, those who were overlooked and ostracised, and those who needed a simple touch to bring wholeness and healing.

Then there are the gifts of love. Gifts that Jesus gave and was glad to receive. Sometimes these gifts were very simple – a cup of water to assuage his thirst[19] – sometimes very extravagant and expensive – a pint of pure nard poured over his head.[20]

My dear friends Allan and Lyn are model givers of love. Having raised their own three children they became foster parents. Their modest Black Country home became a sanctuary of love, peace and healing to a succession of children. From babes in arms to those nearing school age many of them had experienced very difficult starts in life. Whenever I called round there seemed to be a new child being blessed with the gift of a loving home amidst the joyous chaos of bottles and buggies, Telly Tubbies and toddler tantrums.

Allan and Lyn were called to a particular outworking of the adventure of discipleship. They have given so much: their home, their time, their love to create a little bit of heaven in Dudley.

A Transforming Challenge

Of all the holy habits presented by Luke and explored in this book, giving is probably the most challenging. Not least because it challenges most directly the selfishness that is at the heart of many powerful economic systems and which is also the root of personal sinfulness. David Watson used to say that the last part of a person to be converted is the purse or the wallet.

So giving when practised and lived out is truly transformatory, expressing the very essence of God and making the Kingdom real.

Suggestions for Further Reflection and Action

Personally

Seemingly every day we get emails, unsolicited phone calls and mail shots offering to review our insurance or energy bills. But when did we last review our giving in all its forms? Create some time and space to sit with the Spirit and review your giving of money, possessions, time, love and anything else the Spirit draws to your attention.

Read the story of Zacchaeus in Luke 19. Then imagine it is your home Jesus is visiting. What does he give to you? And what do you feel called to give in response?

How can your home be a gift for others?

Locally

How can your local Christian community develop its giving? If you have premises could you host more community groups? To whom could you offer water or food? Could you practise a contemporary community of goods sharing resources and possessions both within the fellowship and with the wider community? When planning the church budget how might you increase giving to others?

Globally

Personally or as a church why not partner with a Christian community in another country and provide them with a regular income stream? Spontaneous gifts are great but regular reliable gifts allow for longer-term planning.

Many are reliant on the gifts of others because they are the victims of unjust economic systems. The Fairtrade movement actively works to redress this. If you are not involved already find out more at fairtarde. org.uk.

A Biblical Passage to Reflect On
- 2 Corinthians 9

What do you notice in this passage?

What will you do or change in the light of what you have read and noticed?

Recommended Reading

- Ian Coffey, *Pennies for Heaven.*
- Peter Johnson and Chris Sugden (eds), *Markets, Fair Trade and the Kingdom of God.*
- Ben Witherington, *Jesus and Money.*

Endnotes

1. Acts 6.
2. Josephus *Jewish War* 2.122.
3. F.F. Bruce, *The Book of the Acts Revised*, Grand Rapids: Erdmans, 1988, p74.
4. James D.G. Dunn, *The Acts of the Apostles*, Peterborough: Epworth, 1996, p36.
5. John Drane, *Introducing the New Testament (Third Edition)*, Oxford: Lion, 2010, p434.
6. Ibid.
7. Ibid.
8. Bradley Blue, 'Acts and the House Church' in D.W.J. Gill and C. Gempf (eds), *The Book of Acts in its First Century Setting*, Carlisle: Paternoster Press, 1994, p141.
9. Ibid, p152.
10. Blue also points out that there were three architectural phases in the early Christian period:
    i. c50–150. Christians met in private homes, belonging to individual members (a practice that may be another taken from Judaism with many contemporary synagogues being rooms in houses).
    ii. c150–250. Private homes were renovated and expanded with rooms used exclusively for the assembled Christian communities.
    iii. c250–313. Larger buildings and halls (both public and private) were used before the introduction of Constantinian basilicas. At this point Holy Communion or Eucharist became more formal and distinct from the holy habit of eating together in the home.
11. Genesis 1:26f; Genesis 2:16f.
12. John 3:16.
13. Deuteronomy 14:22f; Leviticus 27:30–32; etc.
14. Luke 21:1–4.
15. Simon Guillebaud, *More Than Conquerors*, Oxford: Monarch Books, 2009, p142–143.

16. Luke 19:1–10.
17. Proverbs 3:9.
18. freshexpressions.org.uk/views/joining-the-marginalised.
19. Mark 9:41.
20. John 12:3.

13

Service

They would sell their possessions and goods and distribute the proceeds to all, as any had need.

Acts 2:45

When most of us are snuggling under our duvets, dedicated disciples of Jesus are venturing out onto the streets of villages, towns and cities to serve those who may find themselves in need of help. Street Pastors, Street Angels and other similar groups make themselves available to younger people in particular who may be vulnerable, lonely or afraid after a night out that has not ended as they would have hoped. One such group was out in Telford when they met Jaydine[1] one cold and wet November night – at 3am. Overwhelmed by the practical demonstration of Christian love that she encountered, Jaydine wrote this:

Someone to Watch Over Me
Dedicated to Sankj-uary Telford
ow my ears they hurt

'coz the beat's too loud
know I've drunk too much
inside I'm not too proud
lungs can 'ardly breathe
feel like a tub o' lard
no one sees I'm scared
I'm really not that hard
head's spinnin' round 'n round
my heart it's thumpin' fast
whatevah's goin' down
I'm hopin' it won't last
everythin's a blur
don't really wanna stay
to be wiv what occurs
just need to run away
want me mum to hold
so my world won't crash
want me dad to scold
when I am smokin' hash
my god it's freezin' out
how will I make it home
who will take my hand
see that I'm all alone
then I saw your face
glowin' angel bright
offerin' tea and warmth
in the dead of night
you held my eyes
touched my feet with love
wrapped me from the cold
so I wouldn't feel so rough
then I looked again
'n saw my mother's smile
saw my father's pride

not his backhanded bile
I never thought
that I would ever see
someone care enough
to watch over me.

Service is a hallmark of discipleship. It is a Christ-like way of living. Jesus himself pointing out that he came 'not to be served, but to serve'.[2]

Distinctively Christian

As we noted earlier, for Roger Walton, mission (of which service is part) is one of the three key formative energies of discipleship along with worship and intentional community. In *Disciples Together* he helpfully reminds us that we need to be careful not to leave 'the Christ part' out of Christian service, Christian mission.

> It is in and through mission that we are changed by our encounters with others, for it is often in them that we meet the 'otherness' of God. But at the same time Christian mission cannot be a transforming process if we leave out the Christ part. The essential ingredient in the formation of Christian disciples is a relationship with the living Christ. The disciples were involved in mission, and they lived in community together with all the challenges this brought, but all that would not have formed them as followers of Jesus were he not with them.[3]

So it is the presence of Jesus that forms us as disciples as we serve and engage in God's mission and it is the presence of Jesus which is the life-giving distinctive in the service we offer.

Good News

Practising the holy habit of service is an evangelistic act in the literal sense of being good news. It is also so when it opens the way for people to encounter the risen Jesus for themselves and consider his call to follow.

The giving, gladness and generosity of the Acts 2 community was not confined to the fellowship of believers. They didn't just serve one another. Service spilt out onto the streets in acts of kindness and healing. Little wonder then that the church enjoyed

the good will of all the people. And day by day the Lord added to their number those who were being saved.[4]

A Dying Church Reborn

When a Methodist chapel in the Yorkshire village of Howden Clough had dwindled to fewer than ten members the faithful souls who remained decided they needed to have a chat with the community around. 'What do you think of the church?' they asked. They got a bit despondent when someone said, 'What has the church ever done for us except ask for money?' Down but not out they decided to ask a different question, 'How could we serve you?' This was much more fruitful. A range of positive replies came in and the members quickly realised there was a big need for a safe place for children to play and for parents to meet.

One of the members, Caroline (the youngest by many years), took the brave pill and suggested transforming the chapel into a play barn that could serve the community every day of the week. Amazingly the members said yes and, to cut a long story short, that is what they did. Retaining a small area for the traditional worship that the older members still treasure, they converted the rest of the premises into a stunning play centre with a huge soft-play area built in the shape of Noah's Ark, a café and other meeting spaces. And the church enjoyed the good will of the people. Within three years 42,000 people had been through the doors of the missional centre that had been in danger of closing. And whilst it would be an exaggeration to say the Lord added to their number daily those who were being saved, people have come to faith, baptisms have become regular events and regular patterns of prayer and worship have formed in all sorts of creative ways. Looking back over this amazing adventure in discipleship Caroline said:

There is a purpose for every church to be their faith-sharing community and if we're not sharing our faith then why are we here? And perhaps our buildings will be the legacy of the lack of faith that some people have in actually stepping forward and looking to where people need the church and not the other way around.

I would say if anyone's thinking of starting something new – the biggest step is to first let go – let go of the past – let go of all the things that have happened before and actually look forward to what God wants to do through you. So my view is you don't have to be a vicar – you don't have to be a minister – you just have to be a Christian that's willing to follow where Jesus leads.[5]

Incarnational Mission

In Howden Clough the local church reconnected with the community of which it was part. To use some big theological words it engaged in *incarnational mission*. The beginning of John's Gospel celebrates how God in Jesus got involved at first hand in this world. *The Message* translation memorably translates John 1:14 as

The word became flesh and moved into the neighbourhood . . .

Again Jesus is our model. He got involved, walked the streets, sat in the market place, spent time in people's homes. He got his hands dirty and offered the life-changing touch of holiness. He brought heaven down to earth.

The Danger of Disconnection

It is very easy to become disconnected from the neighbourhoods that we are situated in and the communities that we are called to serve. In my previous book *fresh!* I tell this story:

In a small town in the West Midlands, a church had a large day-glow poster advertising an evening of inspirational choral music.

On the other side of the road, directly opposite the notice board, there was a small row of shops with a bookmaker, tattoo shop and chippy lined up adjacently. The road was wide but the cultural gap between the two sides was enormous. Why would anyone placing a tenner on Wayne Rooney to score first, before adding a tattoo to their collection and ending their afternoon with a bag of battered chips[6] cross the road to imbibe the works of John Rutter?[7]

And vice versa of course. This is not to be critical of those who love the works of Rutter or tattoos but to highlight the disconnection that can often exist between the ecclesial community and the wider community of which the church is part.

Reciprocal Hospitality

True service is side by side. It is reciprocal, it is mutual. Speaking about pioneering work, theologian Angie Shier-Jones said:

> Ministry cannot be done to a community by someone who knows what they need, it can only be done with a community by someone who shares their need.[8]

I suggest that this is a word for all authentic and fruitful Christian service (ministry). It needs to be incarnate in, clothed in, sharing the life of, the culture, context and community it is seeking to serve.

Offering hospitality is a way of serving that has been rediscovered in recent years. It is often offered alongside the holy habit of eating together. Writing for the Fresh Expressions course *mission shaped ministry*[9] I suggested that this shouldn't surprise us as there are many instances where hospitality is right at the heart of biblical community engagement:

- the encounter on the road to Emmaus;[10]
- Jesus eating at Levi's house;[11]
- Jesus instructing the seventy on how to engage with those they were sent to;[12]

- Jesus' instruction to invite the poor and needy to the feast;[13]
- The instructions to 'practise hospitality'[14] and show 'hospitality to strangers.'[15]

Writing in the same unit Christian sociologist Ann Morisy argues that:

> Christ-like hospitality is radical action because the 'powerful' host has all the obligations and the vulnerable guest – the stranger – has almost all the rights. True hospitality:
> - is never sold;
> - involves a friendly, caring spirit;
> - is an obligation to be receptive to the guest's needs;
> - is an obligation to hear the guest's story.
>
> True hospitality is reciprocal; the host's role is to learn from the guest – rather than attempt to change the guest. In the offering of a free space, change may take place; however the host must allow the guest the right to remain a stranger and accept the possibility of mystery. True hospitality is also reciprocal in the sense that we need to be open to receive it as well as offering it.

Ann makes an important point here about the offering of all forms of service, including hospitality. It must never be coercive or manipulative. Distinctively Christian? Yes. Loving? Absolutely. But how people respond to the Christ who is at the heart of the service being offered is between Jesus and them.

It is interesting and helpfully reassuring to note how people responded to the service Jesus offered to them. Some did become committed followers. Some were very grateful whilst others just took what they had received and disappeared. This is beautifully illustrated in the story of Jesus' healing of ten people with leprosy.[16] Jesus was delighted when one returned to say thank you but rather perplexed that the other nine couldn't be bothered to come and express their gratitude. After reading this passage a minister once said, 'Lucky old Jesus. I wish ten per cent of the people I helped came back to say thank you.'

Are You Being Served?

God's love is for all. That is one of the great revelations of Acts dramatised by Luke in the story of Peter's conversion to an understanding of God's impartiality.[17] It is a point passionately made by Paul in Galatians:

> *There is no longer Jew or Greek, there is no longer slave or free, there is no longer male and female; for all of you are one in Christ Jesus.*[18]

So God loves black and white, younger and older, the able-bodied and the disabled, rich and poor, and, yes, even bankers, a group of people that have become the object of much opprobrium in recent years not least from Christian people. Now clearly there are some within banking who have betrayed those they serve and their industry and yes there have been structures and systems that have been corrupt. But is there any profession or industry of which this is not true?[19] And there are many, including many faithful disciples of Jesus, working in banks, seeking to be salt and light, serving customers honourably. They need the prayers of communities of faith just as much as those working in healthcare or education.

When it comes to practising the holy habit of service there are no boundaries and if our incarnational zone is the City, or the banking sector, or IT, or professional sport, then let's see how we can serve in a distinctively Christian way there.

A Special Concern for the Poorest

Whilst affirming that God's love is for all, there can be no escaping that in reading through the Bible we see God has a special heart for the poorest in society. It is clear in the laws of the Hebrew Scriptures. Particularly clear in the pronouncements of the prophets. It is abundantly clear in the preaching and teaching of Jesus.

Of all the New Testament writers Luke has perhaps the clearest concern for the poor. This is seen in the 'Nazareth manifesto'[20] in which Jesus declared he has come to 'bring good news to the poor'. It is also powerfully present in Luke's version of the Beatitudes[21] in which he presents Jesus simply saying 'Blessed are the poor' (in contrast to Matthews's version: 'Blessed are the poor in spirit'[22]).

When we get to Luke's portrait of the first Christian community Santos Yao suggests that the promise of Deuteronomy 15:4 is seen to be literally fulfilled. The promise that there shall come a day when 'no one is in need among you'.[23] So the Acts 2 community serves as a prophetic picture of how life, of how society, can be when there is a commitment to service, to give, to be generous – to be Christ-like.

Professor John Hull is one of many who longs to see this prophetic picture reappear in these days. He calls for 'a prophetic church, a church that refuses to accept the poverty which is still so widespread in our society'.[24]

The good news is that in many places the church is acting and living prophetically to counter the forces of poverty that diminish life. As the Fresh Expressions movement develops, examples are emerging of radical communities ministering amongst the most poor economically and inviting them to explore Christian discipleship. In North Wales a fresh expression has been established for the homeless. In York a Christian community has been formed for those with profound addictions, especially drug addictions. The Cable Street Community in Shadwell, East London is bringing the light of the gospel to a soul-destroying tower block estate.

Meanwhile, long-established churches owning the biblical mandate to serve the poorest are responding in imaginative ways and developing new Christian communities. In the small ex-mining town of Hednesford a new congregation has grown around a free lunch provided by the Methodist church. The congregation is made up of homeless people, those with issues of addiction, young single mums and their children. It is a modern version of Luke 14:12–14. Incarnational mission following in the footsteps of the one who came to serve.

Alongside the creation of serving communities that support those in most need directly, there is the ongoing need to act prophetically by supporting those campaigning to eradicate the causes of poverty at home and abroad.

A Holy Muddle

As with all of the holy habits explored in this book, the habit of serving cannot be practised in isolation. It is informed by biblical teaching, supported by fellowship and often involves eating. It is an expression of gladness, generosity and giving, a natural outworking of prayer. As Pope Francis put it, 'You pray for the hungry. Then you feed them. This is how prayer works.'

Suggestions for Further Reflection and Action

Personally

Bless your local bank with some cakes. Let the staff know that someone loves them. You could do this of course for other people and groups that may be under pressure or under-appreciated.

Master or servant? As a disciple of Jesus how do you operate? Take time to ponder this especially if you have a leadership role at work, in the community or in your church. How do you kneel at the feet of those you lead?

Locally

How connected/incarnate is your church within the wider community of which you are part? Is there a neglected or needy part of your community that you might be being called to serve?

If your local Christian community is active in serving the wider community take a little time to reflect on 'the Christ part' of this. How is the service you offer distinctively Christian? How is the presence of Christ revealed in what you do?

Globally

To help serve the poorest renew your commitment to or get involved with an organisation that works to tackle the causes as well as the effects of poverty. There are any number of good organisations that do this but if you are stuck good places to start are:

- Internationally with Christian Aid and its partners who work to bring an end to poverty around the world – tackling its root causes as well as its effects: christianaid.org.uk.
- In the UK the Joint Public Issues Team of the Baptist, Methodist and United Reformed Churches campaigns on issues surrounding poverty and injustice: jointpublicissues.org.uk. So too does the Church Urban Fund: cuf.org.uk.

A Biblical Passage to Reflect On

- Matthew 25:31–46

What do you notice in this passage?

What will you do or change in the light of what you have read and noticed?

Recommended Reading

- Graham Cray, Ian Mobsby and Aaron Kennedy, *Fresh Expression of Church and the Kingdom of God.*
- Ann Morrisey, *Journeying Out.*
- John Hull, *Mission Shaped Church: A Theological Response.*

Endnotes

1. I have changed the name here.
2. Matthew 20:28.
3. Roger L. Walton, *Disciples Together*, London: SCM Press, 2014, p13.
4. Acts 2:47.
5. Norman Ivison, *expressions: making a difference,* Fresh Expressions, 2011, Ch 24. Or freshexpressions.org.uk/resources/makingadifference/24.
6. That is not a proof-reading error, they really do sell battered chips.
7. David Goodhew, Andrew Roberts and Michael Volland, *fresh! An Introduction to Fresh Expressions of Church and Pioneer Ministry*, London: SCM Press, 2012, p110.
8. Angela Shier-Jones, *Pioneer Ministry and Fresh Expressions of Church*, London: SPCK, 2009, p123.
9. Fresh Expressions, *mission shaped ministry*, Unit C06, 'Engaging With Your Community'.
10. Luke 24:13–35.
11. Luke 5:27–32.
12. Luke 10:1–24.
13. Luke 14:12–14.
14. Romans 12:13 NIV.
15. Hebrews 13:2.
16. Luke 17:11–19.
17. Acts 10:34.
18. Galatians 3:28.
19. I write as an ordained minister acutely aware of the terrible things that have been done by some representatives of the Church I serve.

20. Luke 4:18.
21. Luke 6:20.
22. Matthew 5:3.
23. Santos Yao, 'Dismantling Social Barriers Through Table Fellowship' in R.L. Gallagher and P. Hertig, *Mission in Acts*, New York: Orbis, 2004, p33.
24. John Hull, *Mission Shaped Church: a Theological Response*, London: SCM, 2006, p36.

14
Eating Together

Day by day, as they spent much time together in the temple, they broke
bread at home and ate their food with glad and generous hearts.
Acts 2:46

When my friend Norman Ivison produced the first Fresh Expressions DVD,[1] featuring the stories of fourteen newly forming expressions of church, I played and presented the stories all over the UK. After playing a montage of the stories I would ask people what they had noticed in them. Almost always the first answer was 'food', 'people eating together'. In inner-city tower blocks, a British-Asian church, suburban Messy Church, youth churches, student churches, bread-making churches, new rural churches and, of course, café churches. Norman had not set out to film the ecclesiastical equivalent of *Saturday Kitchen* but he filmed what he found. Christians of all ages, in all manner of contexts and cultures, practising the ancient but ever new holy habit of eating together. In so doing they have redeveloped a form of hospitality that is highly missional, inviting others to come and share food and explore faith.

Table Fellowship

Luke was particularly keen to place food and eating together at the heart of discipleship community. In his Gospel there are sixty references to food and drink and ten occasions in which Jesus is seen sharing a meal. Eating together was a key holy habit of the early church. The word 'together' in the habit title reminds us of the corporate nature of discipleship and the habits that nourish and nurture it. Whilst many of the habits can and need to be practised individually they all flourish when practised *together*.

When looking at Holy Habitats we noticed the importance of the home as a place of nurture for the adventure of discipleship. The practice of meeting in homes allowed the early Christians to continue the patterns of table fellowship of Jesus found in the Gospels. As biblical commentator Bradley Blue points out:

> The early believers met in houses *not by default alone* . . . but deliberately because the house setting provided the facilities which were of paramount importance for the gathering. For example, the culinary appurtenances necessary for the meal.[2]

The atmosphere at the shared meals was one of gladness and the believers were characterised by their generous or sincere hearts. The word *aphelotes* occurs here uniquely in the New Testament. It can be translated as either generous or sincere. When translated as sincere it indicates a purity or holiness in the Christian meals that contrasted with the sort of drunkenness of which the Pentecost community was accused in Acts 2:13.

A Heavenly Banquet

People eating together being a sign of God's reign or Kingdom goes way back into the Judaeo-Christian tradition. It is a picture painted by the prophets and celebrated in the psalms:

On this mountain the Lord of hosts will make for all peoples a feast of rich food, a feast of well-matured wines, of rich food filled with marrow, of well-matured wines strained clear.[3]

You prepare a table before me in the presence of my enemies; you anoint my head with oil; my cup overflows.[4]

Jesus was rooted in and lived this tradition. Just as he shared food with all sorts and conditions of people as a sign of the inclusivity of God's Kingdom so, too, did the early church. The gatherings to eat together were down-to-earth representations of the heavenly banquet imagery that had been reinforced by Jesus through his teaching as well as his actions.[5] Following in the footsteps of Jesus, the early Christians refused to discriminate against the marginalised. 'Their table fellowship was characterised by acceptance and egalitarianism.'[6] All were welcome and therein lies a challenge for many a Christian community. How often do we say that in our homes and churches before people experience something different?

A Rediscovered Treasure

The joy of eating together, the value of table fellowship for deepening relationships, the missional fruitfulness of shared meals and the opportunities for sharing faith, biblical study, prayer and worship around the meal table have all been rediscovered in recent years by both new and ancient forms of church. New monasticism places a high value on the sacred experience of eating together. The phenomenon that is Messy Church has a meal as a key ingredient of its programmes. As does the most popular process evangelism course – Alpha. Café worship at its best integrates worship and food whilst Bible study resources such as *Lyfe* produced by the Bible Society have been designed to work around a table sharing food and drink. Churches that work well with students have long realised that the provision of food is a great way to engage with them.

As we noted earlier, fresh expressions of many types have the sharing of food at the heart of their lives. One good example of this is Cook@

Chapel. On the Fresh Expressions website Katharine Crowsley tells how a 'mixing bowl of prayer' has helped to develop this new Christian community.

> Over the past four years Cook@Chapel has grown and evolved as a fresh expression of church. The group of young people meets once a week to cook together, pray together and share a meal. By sharing food, hospitality and worship these young people can develop and deepen their faith – and build a small missional community.
>
> The prayer life of Cook@Chapel has developed very quickly from a grace said at the start of the shared meal to a time of prayer that takes place every week and forms a central focus to our meeting. The young people like to use a kitchen mixing bowl that we place written prayers into; we then pass the bowl around, stirring the prayers and reading them out in turn.[7]

A Multi-dimensional Blessing

Practising the holy habit of eating together provides space in which to practise many of the other holy habits, produces all sorts of blessings and fruit, and fulfils many a biblical mandate. Most simply it fulfils the call of Jesus to feed the hungry.[8] It is an act of Christ-like service and is an end in itself. Jesus himself pointed out that when it comes to eating together we shouldn't restrict the places at the table to those from within our family or fellowship.

> *When you give a banquet, invite the poor, the crippled, the lame, and the blind. And you will be blessed, because they cannot repay you.*[9]

In 2014 nearly 100,000 of the poorest children in the UK went hungry because their parents' benefits were stopped or cut, according to a report by a coalition of churches.[10] Messy Churches and other expressions of Christian community are helping to feed some of these through the practice of eating together.

One of the most memorable Christmas meals I shared was with some homeless men on Princes Street in Edinburgh. I was working in the city a few days before Christmas and went to visit the German market on the garden side of the street. The market was great; alive with light, music, laughter and all sorts of treats to buy and eat. On the other side of the street the homeless men were beginning to bed in for the night, in the cold, in the shop entrances. I went back to the market and got some food and took it across to share with some of the men. It was a holy moment. Their gratitude and smiles were as bright as the lights across the road. As we parted the mutual expressions of 'God bless' were as alive as if the one born outside in a stable whose birth we were celebrating had been physically there pronouncing God's blessing himself.

Eating together can also create safe space in which to share and deepen faith and to offer the invitation to explore the adventure of discipleship. At the meal table we can ask questions and share our stories, needs and struggles. We can celebrate life's joys and rejoice together when we have seen prayers answered and the Kingdom come through our following of Jesus. Eating together also creates a place of belonging where *koinonia* can truly flourish.

And the beauty is that this works in any culture.

When I was working in the Caribbean there was a bank holiday and so I went for a walk. I came to a park where families and church groups were playing cricket and enjoying picnics. I was very obviously not a local (the pale complexion was a giveaway), a total stranger, thousands of miles from home. 'Come over and join us,' came the cry from one group who warmly welcomed me, engaging me in conversation and determinedly plying me with all manner of tasty Bajan treats – the matriarchs in the group seemingly keen to put some fat on my less than muscle bound physique. I had a glorious time. A little bit of heaven in paradise. And I learnt a lot about the value of hospitality, the welcoming of strangers[11] and the sharing of food in building relationships and revealing the Kingdom.

Feasting and Fasting

For deepening discipleship we noted in Chapter 7 the value of living rhythmically. The holy habit of eating together lends itself to a rhythm of life that is both formative of discipleship and missional. Gathering with fellow disciples to celebrate major festivals with the sharing of food has ancient pedigree going deep into our Judaeo-Christian history. Christmas, Easter, Pentecost and Harvest provide quarterly opportunities for eating together with gladness and for inviting others to come and taste and see that the Lord is good.[12]

There is no reason to limit eating together to an occasional event. Many emerging communities gather monthly or weekly to share food and faith. As Mark Berry explains, *safespace* in Telford is one such community that meets each week around the meal table:

> We make and eat a meal, we invite guests to join us, we spend time in reflection and meditation on Scripture, we write, create and use liturgy, we break bread and share wine together, we pray together and we gently and generously hold each other accountable. We have been surprised how vital it has been to eat together as family.[13]

Alongside the habit of feasting and eating together is the ancient faith practice of fasting, abstaining from food for a shorter or longer period, as a sign of devotion, character-building discipline, to create space to pray and explore the Bible. It is a habit that Jesus himself practised.

> Fasting reminds us that we are sustained 'by every word that proceeds from the mouth of God' (Matthew 4:4). In experiences of fasting we are not so much abstaining from food as we are feasting on the word of God. Fasting is feasting![14]

Fasting develops personal holiness. It also contributes to the social holiness of justice. When we fast we identify with those for whom being hungry is not a choice, we stand against the might of the marketers and those who espouse the lie that greed is good. And we can if we choose positively share the resources saved with those who have less.

As well as personal fasting some Christians have practised having very simple, inexpensive meals once a week to identify with the many people around the world who eat simply or not at all, not out of choice but out of necessity or the simple lack of food. The money saved by having such 'hunger lunches' then being given to support those in need elsewhere.

As with feasting, fasting can fit well with a rhythm of life. Many disciples of Jesus practise a weekly day of fasting. Many others consciously practise the habit during Lent. At this time and others fasting does not have to be limited to abstaining from food. We can fast from other things too: from shopping, from social media, from being critical or cynical. Fasting in ways like these can also help to develop personal discipline and holiness. They can also be ways by which we release resources to bless others.

If fasting from food is a habit you have not tried and would like to consider, do make sure that it is safe to do so medically. Have a word with your doctor. You never know, they might be intrigued as to why you want to do it!

Suggestions for Further Reflection and Action

Personally

Take some time to plan a personal twelve-month rhythm of feasting and fasting. Think carefully as to what you would want to achieve through this. Is there a friend you could invite to join you in this?

Rediscover the home as a place of discipleship and make eating together part of this through daily practices such as praying over the day's events at meal times or through a weekly feast of thanksgiving for the blessing you have enjoyed that week.

Locally

Within your church plan some times to eat together. Take care to think through the purpose of the meals you plan. Are they primarily an invitational opportunity? A gift to the community – perhaps inviting the housebound, homeless and others to a Kingdom banquet? Or are they a time to deepen fellowship and share in prayer?

How can you make use of the opportunities presented by the major festivals and develop them as times of community feasting?

Globally

To help develop global-local relationships invite others from different countries, ethnicities or cultures to share their favourite food with you.

To practice social holiness consider following the example of Cook@ Chapel and teach local children how to cook and pray.

Using the resources freely available from charities such as Christian Aid or Tearfund arrange simple community lunches at which people can reflect upon needs in other parts of the world and give in support of these.

A Biblical Passage to Reflect On

• Luke 14:15–23

What do you notice in this passage?

What will you do or change in the light of what you have read and noticed?

Recommended Reading

- Dilly Baker, *Liturgies and Resources for Christ-centred Hospitality.*
- Sylvia Hart, *Extending the Table, A World Community, Cookbook, Friends, Faith and Feasts.*
- Leonard Sweet, *From Tablet to Table.*

Endnotes

1. Norman Ivison, *expressions: the dvd – 1: stories of church for a changing culture*, Church House Publishing, 2006.

2. Bradley Blue, *Acts and the House Church* in D.W.J. Gill and C. Gempf (eds), *The Book of Acts in its First Century Setting*, Carlisle: Paternoster Press, 1994, p121.

3. Isaiah 25:6.

4. Psalm 23:5.

5. Luke 14:14–24.

6. Santos Yao, 'Dismantling Social Barriers Through Table Fellowship' in R.L. Gallagher and P. Hertig, *Mission in Acts*, New York: Orbis, 2004, p33.

7. freshexpressions.org.uk/stories/cookatchapel/apr13.

8. Matthew 25:31–46.

9. Luke 14:13–14.

10.independent.co.uk/life-style/health-and-families/health-news/nearly-100000-of-britains-poorest-children-go-hungry-after-parents-benefits-are-cut-10079056.html.

11. Someone pointed out to me recently that the command to love your neighbour occurs once in the Old Testament whereas the command to love the stranger occurs twenty-seven times.

12. Psalm 34:8.

13. Ian Mobsby and Mark Berry, *A New Monastic Handbook*, Norwich: Canterbury Press, 2014, p178.

14. Richard Foster, *Celebration of Discipline*, London: Hodder and Stoughton, 1989, p70.

15
Gladness and Generosity

Day by day, as they spent much time together in the temple, they broke
bread at home and ate their food with glad and generous hearts.
Acts 2:46

Surrounded by giant bananas, a group of 'nuns' and the characters
from Scooby Doo, my son Matt and I danced and sang with euphoric
gladness (and a touch of disbelief) as the England cricket team powered
to a record-breaking win over New Zealand at Edgbaston. The raucous
rendition of 'Sweet Caroline' by a choir of thousands was particularly
amazing with complete strangers harmonising with new friends.

Moments of such extreme gladness are of course rare, particularly if
you support England. But they are wonderful when they come and to
be enjoyed, cherished and remembered. Both the experience and the
memory are energising, life-giving.

Pentecost Joy
The atmosphere in Jerusalem was euphoric when the promise of Jesus

was fulfilled as the Spirit was poured out upon the disciples on the day of Pentecost. Sometimes, often, the divine is experienced in quietness and the still small voice but that day the holy encounter was one of noise and colour and drama as the party of all parties began.

> *Suddenly from heaven there came a sound like the rush of a violent wind, and it filled the entire house where they were sitting. Divided tongues, as of fire, appeared among them, and a tongue rested on each of them. All of them were filled with the Holy Spirit and began to speak in other languages, as the Spirit gave them ability.*[1]

The church was born in gladness. Gladness for what God had done through the life, death and resurrection of Jesus and the outpouring of the Spirit as promised long ago by the prophets and explained by Peter in his Pentecost address. There was gladness in the home, gladness in the temple and gladness out on the streets.

James Dunn in his book *Jesus and the Spirit* argues that 'eschatological enthusiasm' played a key part in the formation and life of the first Christian communities and has been a key factor in the birth of renewal and missionary movements ever since. Reflecting on Acts 2:44f and Acts 4:32–37 he writes:

> These considerations make it quite clear both the fact and the character of the eschatological enthusiasm which gripped the earliest Jerusalem community. This enthusiasm was a direct experience of Spirit. The link between enthusiasm and expectation of an imminent *parousia* [return of Jesus] is a recurring feature of the history of Christianity from Pentecost to Pentecostalism.[2]

He also warns against the dual dangers of being dependent upon or dismissive of ecstatic, euphoric spiritual experience.

A preacher was once visiting a church and was told in no uncertain manner by a grim-faced steward that his church did not do any of this 'enthusiastic happiness'. Theirs was a deep joy. Having endured an hour of their deep joy the preacher encouraged the gathering to send a message from the depths of their joy to their faces as a smile or two would not go amiss. And with that he promptly left.

A Comprehensive Gladness

Gladness is experienced and expressed in many ways. On the adventure of discipleship there are moments when gladness is ecstatic. Mountain-top moments marvelling at the goodness of God in creation or singing in your mother tongue or other languages with thousands of fellow disciples. It can be known in deeply personal moments of sexual intimacy or heart-warming friendship. When a child is born or a massive injustice is overcome. There was gladness a-plenty when the Berlin Wall came down and separated peoples were reunited.

There are other times when gladness is more plodding and pedestrian. Literally so when out walking and delighting in all that is going on around. Metaphorically so when exercising a healing ministry by caring for the patients on the ward, harvesting the crops, finding the source of the annoying misfire in the car being serviced or teaching truculent teenagers that maths will be useful to them one day.

There are still other times when gladness goes deep, very deep. When gladness strengthens and sustains, brings tranquillity and transformation in the darkest of places. We encountered such gladness in the story of Joy in Chapter 4. I have been privileged to encounter many other such examples.

I once met with a widow to plan the funeral service of her husband. She told me of the night he died following a long illness. Knowing this would probably be their final evening together the lady did her makeup and hair and put on her finest nightie. They poured a glass of champagne and got out their photo albums. Then cuddling up under the duvet they looked back with gladness over the life they had shared together whilst looking forward to the fullness of heaven that would soon be the husband's experience.

The gladness of that moment is one the lady will always treasure. A gladness that was her strength in the darkness of her grief.

A Habit to be Practised

Like all of the other habits in this book, gladness is a gift of the Spirit but also one we can choose to receive and one that we need to practise. It is a holy, transformatory gift for the individual, the church and the world.

In an age when many are anxious about the future, gladness can change the landscape. In a prescient and prophetic piece, GP and former Vice President of the British Methodist Conference Richard Vautrey suggests that any Christian communities concerned that time may be against them should adopt the kind of attitude wonderfully demonstrated by the inspirational Stephen Sutton[3] and have fun whilst living life to the max with whatever time is left, giving away as much as possible. And of course there is a glorious godly irony in this; for any church that is marked by generosity and knows how to party as well as how to pray, may well not die at all.

Patients who know they are going to die often have a very different outlook on life. They make the most of every precious day. Yes, they prepare and put their affairs in order, but many also compile bucket lists of exciting and challenging things to do whilst they have the strength and energy to do them. They do things they never thought themselves capable of.

So let's not dwell on our pain but instead celebrate each God-given day we have left. Let's not worry too much about long, detailed plans and being too 'methodical', let's instead experiment, take risks and have fun whilst we do so. Let's share our joy for life with those around us and let's spend the inheritance saved up by the saints who have gone before us, not with a sense of gloom as we mourn our own loss, but with joy and gratitude for the generosity of an ever-present God.[4]

Gladness and Generosity

In his cameo portrait of the early adventurous Christian communities

Luke notes that they had glad and generous hearts. The holy habitats embodied the extravagant generosity that is at the heart of the divine Trinitarian community. They were prophetic counter-cultural symbols in a world of avarice and greed.

There are so many ways in which godly generosity can be practised today. Through the language we use to express support and thanks (don't rush that email or text – pause to add some generous encouragement). Through radical generosity that makes people truly welcome. Through the ways in which we open and share our homes and families with those who lovingly foster and adopt children being outstanding examples of generous living.

All of the holy habits can be practised and lived with generosity. In Chapter 12, when exploring the holy habit of giving, we noted the generosity that marked the giving of the first communities of disciples. When it comes to generous giving there are many ways in addition to financial ways that we can give graciously. The gift of forgiveness being the most poignant and powerful.

Forgiveness and Reconciliation

At the very heart of the Christian gospel and life is the immeasurably generous message and act of forgiveness and reconciliation, expressed through the sending of the Father, the self-giving of the Son and the infilling of the Spirit. The theologians call it atonement – at-one-ment.

When we embark on the adventure of discipleship as children of God, followers of Jesus and vessels of the Holy Spirit, we are called to a life of generosity. And the most wonderful and challenging way in which we can express that generosity is by practising forgiveness and reconciliation. These are truly holy, life-giving and transformational practices.

Some of the most vivid examples of these practices in recent history have been seen and experienced in central and southern Africa. Most notably in South Africa and Rwanda. South Africa was a broken and divided nation in which the majority had been abused and oppressed by the minority. Led by Nelson Mandela and Desmond Tutu the country chose to look to a future of reconciliation and hope via the pathways of truth, forgiveness and reconciliation.

In Rwanda nearly a million people were massacred in three months of 1994. Many of them were previously close friends and neighbours. Since that tragic time the most extraordinary stories have emerged of generosity being exercised by way of forgiveness and reconciliation. In her stunning book *Left to Tell* Immaculée Ilibagiza tells of the day she came face to face with Felicien, a man she had known from childhood and with whose children she had played. A man who went on to murder her mother (Rose) and butcher her brother (Damescene) in the Rwandan genocide.

His dirty clothing hung from his emaciated frame in tatters. His skin was sallow, bruised, and broken; and his eyes were filmed and crusted. His once handsome face was hidden beneath a filthy, matted beard; and his bare feet were covered in open, running sores.

I wept at the sight of his suffering. Felicien had let the devil enter his heart, and the evil had ruined his life like a cancer in his soul. He was now the victim of his victims, destined to live in torment and regret. I was overwhelmed with pity for the man.

'He looted your parents' home and robbed your family's plantation, Immaculée. We found your dad's farm machinery at his house, didn't we?' Semana yelled at Felicien. 'After he killed Rose and Damescene, he kept looking for you . . . he wanted you dead so he could take over your property.'

I flinched, letting out an involuntary gasp. Semana looked at me, stunned by my reaction and confused by the tears streaming down my face. He grabbed Felicien by the shirt collar and hauled him to his feet. 'What do you have to say to Immaculée?'

Felicien was sobbing. I could feel his shame. He looked up at me for only a moment, but our eyes met. I reached out, touched his hands lightly, and quietly said what I'd come to say.

'I forgive you.'[5]

Generous seems too small a word to describe such an act. Such forgiveness also puts into sharp relief the resentments and bitterness that too often we refuse to lay down from experiences way less serious than those in this story. From the beautiful and slowly healing land of Rwanda, Immaculée says to us:

> Anyone in the world can learn to forgive those who have injured them, however great or small that injury may be.[6]

Follow Me

As followers of the one who cried 'Father, forgive them; for they do not know what they are doing',[7] forgiveness is an imperative part of our calling. It is part of the cross we take up as we follow, and live out the adventure of discipleship in all the joys, hassles and challenges of daily life and work.

> Then he said to them all, 'If any want to become my followers, let them deny themselves and take up their cross daily and follow me.[8]

Forgiveness is part of a generous life. And generosity is a truly holy habit to be struggled with, lived and shared. It is key to a just, peaceful and glad world.

Gladness and Generosity Create Goodwill

In his cameo of the first Christian communities, Luke notes that those first adventuring disciples had 'the good will of all the people'.[9] Is it any wonder when they were full of gladness and generosity? These habits are infectious, encouraging positivity and reciprocity in others.

In recent years some of the most generous people I have encountered have been Street Pastors. Sacrificially and gladly giving of their time when many of us are cuddling our hot chocolates, to show God's love on the streets, caring for young people fragile and vulnerable in town and city centres late at night. Their generosity has been noted and appreciated by many. In Perth the A&E department of the local hospital was so grateful for the work of the Street Pastors, which reduced admissions for them, that they made a significant gift to support the work of those dedicated disciples.

Gladness, generosity, goodwill. It's a godly way of life.

Suggestions for Further Reflection and Action

Personally

Take some time to reflect on your practising of gladness. If life is tough at the moment and gladness seems elusive, spend some time with someone who is in a tough place at the moment and maybe give them a simple gift such as cake or flowers. Often a good way to regain gladness is to give gladness.

Stories such as those of Immaculée challenge us to let go of the resentments that damage relationships and harm us too. Spend some time simply praying the lines from the Lord's Prayer: 'forgive us our sins as we forgive those who sin against us'. As you pray them slowly, over and over, ask the Spirit to give you the grace to forgive those who have hurt you.

Locally

Why not follow Richard Vautrey's advice (even if you are part of a thriving community) and go a bit crazy with a big extravagant party.

In the more mundane but necessary world of meetings at work, at church or at any club you are part of, get into the habit of auditing the decisions that are made. Keep asking: are they as generous as they can possibly be?

Globally

Personally or in your community adopt a project that is committed to putting a smile on the faces of others or fostering forgiveness and reconciliation. There are many, many good charities that could help with this. If you are stuck for ideas:

- Smile Train literally helps to put a smile on people's faces www. smiletrain.org.uk.
- PHARP (Peace, healing and reconciliation project) is developing all of these in Rwanda www.pharp.org.

A Biblical Passage to Reflect On

- Psalm 100

What do you notice in this passage?

What will you do or change in the light of what you have read and noticed?

Recommended Reading

- Michael Henderson, *Forgiveness: Breaking the Chain of Hate*.
- Immaculée Ilibagiza, *Left to Tell*.
- Philip Yancey, *What's So Amazing About Grace?*

Endnotes

1. Acts 2:2–4.
2. James D.G. Dunn, *Jesus and the Spirit*, London: SCM Press, 1975, p161.
3. www.facebook.com/StephensStory.
4. *Methodist Recorder* 20 June, 2014.
5. Immaculée Ilibagiza, *Left to Tell*, London: Hay House, 2007, p263.
6. Ibid, p270.
7. Luke 23:34.
8. Luke 9:23.
9. Acts 2:47.

16
Worship

*Day by day, as they spent much time together in the temple, they
broke bread at home and ate their food with glad and generous hearts,
praising God and having the good will of all the people.*
Acts 2:46–47

We sat in box pews so angular and rigid they could have been a medieval
instrument of torture. I was eighteen at the time and having read so much
about this exciting church at the cutting edge of charismatic renewal I
was shocked when the clergy came in wearing their traditional robes
and surprised when, flicking through the service book, I found it full of
traditional prayers and liturgy. I quickly checked that I was in the right
place and then the service began. It lasted two hours. But it could have
been five minutes. A transfixing, transforming, glorious time of wonder,
love and praise. Full of life, creativity and a tangible sense of the Spirit in
the midst, I made my way back to my university halls hungry for more
just like those first disciples gathered in Jerusalem. I was blessed to spend
three years worshipping at St Michael-le-Belfrey in York.

A Community Full of Worship and Praise

The holy habit of worship is, like prayer, a prominent theme in Luke's writings. The first story he tells in his Gospel is set in the context of worship. In the midst of this Zechariah receives the news that his prayers have been heard and that he and Elizabeth are to have a son, John.[1] The Gospel concludes with the story of Jesus' ascension, with the disciples worshipping him before returning to Jerusalem where 'they were continually in the temple blessing God'.[2]

So it is no surprise that when Luke's second volume unfurls we find worship at the heart of the nascent church in Jerusalem. Spirit-filled, exuberant praise offered in the home, the temple and on the streets – in public and in private. In his writings Luke presents people praising God[3] in response to experiencing God's loving help or saving grace. Praise and worship flow from gratitude and thanksgiving for who God is and what God has done.

Worship: a Way of Life

There is a risk when it comes to worship that we think of it only as something that is done when Christians gather together for an hour or two a week. Whilst gatherings are good, and certainly a habit to be encouraged, there is so much more to worship than this. Biblically, worship is a way of life. A way of life encapsulated in the Jewish *Shema* – a prayer which is the centre piece of Jewish morning and evening prayer services. It includes these words from Deuteronomy 6:5:

> Love the LORD your God with all your heart, and with all your soul, and with all your might.

Worship offered as grateful response for all God is and does involves all of our lives: our work, our rest, our enjoyment of creation, our service, our eating, our giving – and, yes, our gatherings with fellow disciples for the focused activity of praise and worship. So tending the crops, or forming an algorithm, or building a house, or serving a customer can all be done as acts of worship to the glory of God and the blessing of his creation. As can the celebration of the Eucharist, the singing of songs, the offering of dance, sculpture or art and the praying of prayers.

Worship: an Expression of Devotion

In the New Testament there are a number of different Greek words that are translated into English as 'worship'. By far the most common word is *proskyneo*. The root meaning of *proskyneo* is 'to come towards and kiss the back of the hand'. So it speaks of an act of devotion, humility, intimacy and reverence. It also speaks of an amazing grace and generosity on the part of a Holy God that not just permits but encourages ordinary everyday people like you and me, struggling to be holy, to worship in this way.

For me the passage that most vividly demonstrates this understanding of worship is ironically one that does not feature the word *proskyneo*. It is the story of the anointing of Jesus by a woman who is anonymous in Matthew's[4] and Mark's[5] accounts and named as Mary the sister of Martha and brother of Lazarus in John's[6] telling of the story (the second irony here is that Luke does not have this story in his Gospel). The anointing is an act expressing the deepest devotion and love. It is a prophetic act, anticipating Jesus' death. It is a symbolic act. A humble act. A creative act. A deeply personal, intimate act. A fragrant act of worship that engaged many of the senses. And it is a costly, sacrificial act. Costly financially and costly personally, with 'Mary' tragically having to endure the scorn of those who did not approve of the way she offered her worship (sadly an experience that has too often been replicated over the years by those who should know better).

As part of a worshipping way of life there need to be poignant, passionate moments. When either alone or as part of a crowd, worship is focused in a deep way, an intimate way, a way that touches the purity and holiness of love as it did that day when the fragrance of perfume filled the air.

Worship: a Formative Energy

The holy encounter of 'Mary' anointing Jesus was for her a formative, a transformative, moment. How affirmed she must have felt when Jesus, silencing the moaners and the critics, said, 'Leave her alone . . . She has performed a good service for me.'[7] Her act of worship was also transformed by Jesus into a missional act, an evangelistic act, as he declared:

> Truly I tell you, wherever the good news is proclaimed in the whole world, what she has done will be told in remembrance of her.[8]

For Roger Walton, worship is one of the key formative energies of discipleship, together with mission and intentional community. In *Disciples Together* he helpfully points out the argument of James Smith that 'we become like the things we most love and desire'.[9] This, of course, has been said of pet-lovers for years. More importantly in worship 'our attentiveness to God and our expressions of love towards the divine are inevitably shaping who we are'.[10] Roger then goes on to suggest:

> God is continually acting in forming the created order and all creatures within it. Thus at a moment of openness to God, which worship represents, God's grace has a special opportunity to form and transform us.[11]

An opportunity encapsulated in words by the simple, timeless, worship song 'Spirit of the Living God':

Spirit of the living God,

Fall afresh on me.

Break me, melt me, mould me, fill me.

Spirit of the living God,

Fall afresh on me.[12]

A Rhythm of Worship

Together with biblical teaching and prayer, worship is a holy habit that needs to be lived rhythmically. All three permeate the whole of life: biblical teaching informing and guiding, prayer being the spiritual air we breathe and true worship being a way of life, but all three need their regularly focused moments: daily, weekly, at festival times.

In a book about discipleship formation it is important not to forget that worship is first and foremost a gift we offer to the divine community of the Holy Trinity. We do so in honour of who God is and in love and gratitude for the life and blessings we have received – hence the emphasis on devotion above. It is not that God neurotically needs our worship, but rather that God, as the Psalms remind us, both delights in[13] and in a mystical way inhabits the praises of his people.[14]

In any healthy loving relationship there needs to be regular times at which those who are committed to each other affirm their love and commitment. We need to beware of becoming like the down-to-earth, plain-speaking Yorkshireman who in response to his wife's lament that he never told her that he loved her said, 'I told you the day we were married that I loved you. And if the situation should ever change I'll let you know.'

So personally it is important to have daily moments set aside for worship. If time and circumstances permit it is good to have a space in our home or garden or maybe a nearby field or park to which we can go and offer our worship and praise. If life is full on and hectic then we can worship as we commute, letting the Spirit guide us into praise as we look around and see an electricity pylon speaking to us of the power of God, a baby in a buggy speaking of the new life that God gives, or the sun setting in golden glory reminding us of the majesty and splendour of God.

As well as developing personal practices of praise and worship it is also healthy, biblical and important to set aside times to gather with fellow disciples to worship the one who calls us and unites us. As Alison Morgan cleverly reminds us in the title of her book, *The Plural of Disciple is Church*.[15] The root meaning of the Greek word *ecclesia* that we translate into English as 'church' is 'gathering'.

In his 2015 Lambeth lecture, Archbishop Justin Welby said this:

I want to start by saying just two simple sentences about the church. First, the church exists to worship God in Jesus Christ.

Second, the church exists to make new disciples of Jesus Christ.

Everything else is decoration. Some of it may be very necessary, useful, or wonderful decoration – but it's decoration.[16]

Now Archbishop Justin did go on to point out there are many other things that it is important to be involved with including campaigning for social justice and working for reconciliation. Rhetorically, however, he was making a strong point that the holy habit of worship has a primacy in the life of disciples together.

Worship is important in smaller gatherings which naturally lend themselves to an intimacy and depth in worship. Worship is important in larger gatherings with a particular devotional and formational energy to be found in crowds gathering for festivals. And worship is important in *all* gatherings of disciples together whether it be for focused acts of worship, missional adventures – from going out with the Street Pastors to climbing Kilimanjaro – or the apparently routine and mundane business of property committees. Let worship fragrance these gatherings too and see the difference time focused on worship produces! As Paul puts it in Colossians:

Whatever you do, in word or deed, do everything in the name of the Lord Jesus, giving thanks to God the Father through him.[17]

Who We Are is How We Worship

When exploring prayer we noted how there are many different ways in which followers of Jesus prefer to practise that holy habit, much of this being related to our character, temperament and personality. The same is true when it comes to worship.

I once went to a Christian conference in Birmingham. It was a good conference but there was one worship song that we sang several times every day that drove me nuts. It was called 'Come Help Change the World' and had a ponderous chorus line 'Hallelujah, Maranatha' that was repeated ad infinitum and droned on and on and on. A cat scraping its nails on a chalk board would have been more enjoyable.

I was a very grumpy and reluctant worshipper.

A few months later I was idly browsing through some magazines when I met my friend Keith staring at me from the cover of a mission periodical. He was crouched next to an African child. Intrigued I found the associated article and discovered that Keith had felt called to go to Africa after attending a conference. In Birmingham. At which they had sung this 'wonderful' song 'Come Help Change the World'.

'I couldn't sing that wonderful song and not go,' said Keith.

That taught me. I might not like a particular style or way of worshipping but if it helps another to express their worship and transforms them, and through them, the world, then Hallelujah – quite literally.

Candles and Chainsaws

Some years later I attended a seminar exploring different forms of worship. The leader was carefully introducing a range of ways in which worship could be led or curated with a view to helping those new to the practice of worship express their thoughts and feelings in adoration and praise. The ideas were introduced well and many in the room were appreciative. But there was one man who was getting more and more exasperated as a host of reflective ways of worship were introduced, many involving candles. Finally he could contain himself no more and cried out, 'I can't be doing with all this touchy feely stuff! I like to express my worship with my chainsaw!' He did go on to point out that he liked to create large sculptures with his power tool to express his worship.

I've never forgotten that seminar, not least because of the stunned reaction to the thought of using a chainsaw in worship. But I remember it, too, as a reminder for those who lead gathered worship of how vital it is to take care when creating or curating worship events to allow all those present to express their thoughts, feelings and emotions. There is a particular challenge here in creating worship events that don't inadvertently exclude men. Why is it that worship services in the UK at least are typically one-third male and two-thirds female?

Spiritual Styles

Creating worship events is a complex task. There are matters of culture, age and resources to be taken into account. Then there are character and personality issues to be considered.

Drawing on the insights of research into learning styles and personality types, Canadian research student and practitioner Dave Csinos has identified four primary 'spiritual styles' through which worshippers connect most readily with God, their environment and their fellow worshippers. He names the styles as Word, Emotion, Symbol and Action.[18]

Those who are predominantly 'Word' find it most helpful to express worship through carefully structured worship with written material. 'Emotional' people prefer worshipping in groups, creatively and in ways that express feelings. 'Symbolic' people often prefer worshipping alone, through art or symbols and outside by encountering God in nature. 'Action' people want to make connections between worship and life, welcome people and be part of worship events that lead to missional activity.

Care in the Creation

Reading the stories of creation in the context of thinking about worship I am struck by two things. The first is the care in both the story-telling of Genesis 1 and 2, and in the creative activity of God that is described. There is careful thought, planning and arranging. The second thing that strikes me is the goodness and quality of that which is created. I love the writers repeated phrase:

God saw that it was good.[19]

I imagine God like a great artist stepping back from the easel, quietly taking pleasure in that which has been created.

For God's sake we need to take care in creating and offering worship. God is worthy of the very best we can offer. As are those with whom we gather. Whether it be at choral evensong in a great cathedral, or at a skateboard park like Legacy XS[20] where young people weave patterns and land tricks on their boards and BMX bikes to the glory of God. Whether it be in the noise and bustle of Messy Church or the quiet contemplation of a new monastic community gathered on a beach. Or whether it be in the club dance rhythms of the Transcendence Mass,[21] the worship band led celebrations of a student church or the lusty singing of Wesley hymns, God and those gathered deserve the best that can be offered.

So healthy and helpful focused worship events will take care to create opportunities for all of these styles to be engaged with and expressed. They will take care to engage with all of the senses utilising taste, touch and fragrance as well as sight and sound. And like expressions all of the other holy habits done well, they will connect with the creativity of God. They will be adventurous, colourful, Spirit filled, alive!

Suggestions for Further Reflection and Action

Personally

Review your rhythm of worship. How could you begin or refresh a daily pattern of worship? To what extent is worship a way of life for you?

Take some time to experience worship in different forms and from different traditions. Take a look at what some fresh expressions are doing. Note what you discover to be helpful and build that into your own patterns of worship. Practise being generous in your attitude towards styles of worship that you personally find less helpful.

Locally

Reflect on the focused worship offered by any church community that you are part of. How creative is it? Or is the same thing offered without imagination? Does it engage all the senses or just one or two? How does it cater for a range of spiritual styles?

How are children and young people being nurtured to practise the holy habit of worship? Are they passive recipients or active participants? How might their gifts, insights and natural sense of wonder be a blessing to others?

Practise weaving worship into all of your church meetings. A worship centre with symbols can be really helpful here. Try lighting a candle, placing a cross or a bowl and towel in the middle of your business meetings and see how these symbols of worship and service change the atmosphere in the meeting.

Globally

Take some time to experience worship with people of different languages, nationalities and ethnicities. Note how the work of the Spirit transcends language and culture.

Draw on the songs, liturgies and worship practices of other cultures and contexts. Have a go at dancing to African drums or Caribbean rhythms. Sing in Spanish. Rediscover the riches of the Celtic traditions.

A Biblical Passage to Reflect On

- Deuteronomy 6:4–9

What do you notice in this passage?

What will you do or change in the light of what you have read and noticed?

Recommended Reading

- Jonny Baker, *Curating Worship*.
- Graham Kendrick, *Worship*.
- Sue Wallace, *Multi-sensory Worship*.

Endnotes

1. Luke 1:5–13.
2. Luke 24:53.
3. Luke 2:13,20; 19:37; Acts 3:8; etc.
4. Matthew 26:6–13.
5. Mark 14:3–9.
6. John 12:1–8.
7. Mark 14:6.
8. Mark 14:9.
9. James K.A. Smith, *Desiring the Kingdom: Worship, Worldview, and Cultural Formation*, Grand Rapids: Baker Academic, 2009.
10. Roger L. Walton, *Disciples Together*, London: SCM Press, 2014, p17.
11. Ibid.
12. 'Spirit of the Living God' written by Daniel Iverson © 1963 Birdwing Music (administered by CapitolCMGPublishing.com / UK and Eire Song Solutions www.songsolutions.org). All rights reserved. Used by permission.
13. Psalm 149:4.
14. Psalm 22:3 King James Version.
15. Alison Morgan, *The Plural of Disciple is Church*, Wells; Resource, 2015.
16. archbishopofcanterbury.org/articles.php/5515/lambeth-lectures-archbishop-justin-on-evangelism-video.
17. Colossians 3:17.
18. David's research has been used and developed by the ecumenical worship resources ROOTs for Worship rootsontheweb.com.
19. Genesis 1:12,18,21,25,31.
20. legacyxs.com.
21. freshexpressions.org.uk/stories/visions.

17
Making More Disciples

And day by day the Lord added to their number those who were being saved.
Acts 2:47

The passage of Acts 2:42–47 from which we have been exploring our ten holy habits ends with a summary sentence that highlights the core theme of the book of Acts, namely the spread of the word of God and the growth in the number of followers of Jesus. Implicit in the passage is the message that a deep and committed Christian community which lives out the holy habits is a powerful witness to the reality of the saving love of God. As David Watson puts it, 'It is not surprising with such a community of disciples bound together in love that God added to their number, day by day, those who were being saved.'[1]

An Holistic Salvation
When working for Fresh Expressions I came across Norma who heard the call of Jesus to the adventure of discipleship through Mind the Gap, a Fresh Expression in Gateshead based on a cell church model.

Norma shared her story:

> I became a follower of Jesus three years ago. I had a drink problem, my home was full of violence and rage. Three months after asking Jesus to come into my life, I was controlling my drinking habits. Three months after that I was not drinking at all. I have my family back, my home is now filled with love and hope and peace in Jesus.

Norma's story is one that movingly illustrates the wonder and depth of God's saving work experienced in response to the call of Jesus to follow. Biblically 'being saved' is so much more than getting our cards stamped for heaven. Essentially it is about being made whole; being reconciled to God, oneself and others, set free from the selfishness of sin to live a life of gladness, generosity and self-giving and participating in the Kingdom work of justice, healing, reconciliation and peace for all creation.

Luke Wardle knows what a profound and deep experience this is. Telling his story to Fresh Expressions he said:

> Life before I met Paul and Elaine Little, who run the Grafted project [at Newcastleton in the Scottish Borders] was pretty shocking to be honest. When I was 13 years old I started smoking cannabis and then by the time I was 14 I had started to become a dealer, selling quite large amounts for my age at the time, and really the draw of money and power, respect was quite high. I very quickly became addicted and started to work my way up the ladder taking harder drugs.
>
> Eventually when I was like 19 I ended up with a really bad cocaine habit. I had a heart attack at the age of 20 induced by an overdose and then, shortly after that, I started taking heroin. I was addicted to heroin for about a year and then I got put on the methadone for two years and to be honest it really wasn't much of what I would call a life, it wasn't really living. I got to the stage where I really feel that God actually brought me to such a level where I had no other

option but to cry out to him and ask for his forgiveness. And being with Paul and Elaine and the rest of the people on the project, they actually helped me through my withdrawals when I decided to come off methadone. They prayed me through it and I do know for a fact that it was nowhere near as bad as what it should have been and that was the power of God working in my life to help me through that struggle.

I've now got my qualification for walking so I'm a leader in that and my mountain biking, I can lead that as well. My father now lives in Australia. Once I have enough qualifications, I would really like to move out to Australia and be an evangelist over there through outdoor activities such as mountain biking and hill walking. I really feel that it would be a great way for me to get the message of the gospel across to people so I'm really looking forward to visiting a new country, especially one that is going to be sunny![2]

Getting Heaven into People

When discussing the aims of discipleship I suggested that the big picture aim of discipleship is the transformation of the world. For the Kingdom of heaven to be real on earth. It is important to bear this in mind when seeking to make disciples. Steve Hollinghurst in his very helpful book *Mission Shaped Evangelism* argues that making disciples is 'not first about getting people into heaven but getting heaven into people.'[3] Expressing concern about proclaiming what he calls a 'partial gospel' focused on the forgiveness of the individual and his or her access to heaven Steve suggests that:

> While it is good news for those asking questions about the next life or feeling the weight of guilt, it provides a very questionable motive for following Christ; it encourages us to do so purely for selfish ends and to treat faith as an insurance policy.[4]

He does not dispute the importance of either forgiveness or heaven or the central place of the atoning death and resurrection of Jesus for both of these but he does suggest that:

> In the Western church too much emphasis has been placed on getting into heaven to the detriment of how we are called to live on earth.[5]

To live on earth in a way that embraces, embodies and displays the Kingdom of heaven. To demonstrate that we are truly following Jesus by living with Christ-like character. To live life that blesses others.

The Process of Salvation

In describing the new disciples who were being added to the early Christian community Luke says they were being saved. The use of the present participle emphasises that salvation is a process of which repentance, initial belief, baptism and the gift of the Spirit are only the start. It is a process of transformation to a life of holiness that continues in community. There is no solitary Christianity here. Those who are being saved are added by the Lord to the community which, guided by the apostles' teaching and the Spirit, continues his mission and ministry – and grows.

A Divine Commission

The community of believers that we encounter in Acts was living out a divine commission given by Jesus to his first disciples and recorded by Matthew at the end of his Gospel.

> *Go therefore and make disciples of all nations, baptising them in the name of the Father and of the Son and of the Holy Spirit, and teaching them to obey everything that I have commanded you.[6]*

The verb *matheteuo* (make disciples) occurs three times in the New Testament.[7] The use of the word by Jesus in Matthew has had an enormous impact on Christian mission. Steven Croft puts it this way:

> If ever a single verse could be said to have shaped the history of

the world, this is the one. We should be careful as we weigh it and interpret it for today.[8]

In English translations of the passage known as the Great Commission[9] there are four verbs:

1. Go;
2. Make disciples;
3. Baptise;
4. Teach.

In the Greek there is one imperative verb which governs the other three: 'make disciples' (one word in Greek). In Matthew's Gospel the making of disciples was the prime objective given to the followers of Jesus. In Matthew 16:18 we find Jesus saying to Peter, 'I will build my church.' It is Jesus' job to build the church and ours to make disciples. How often do we assume it is the other way round?

Luke has a different commissioning story to that recorded by Matthew. In the first chapter of Acts he presents the risen Jesus saying to the disciples:

You will receive power when the Holy Spirit has come upon you; and you will be my witnesses in Jerusalem, in all Judea and Samaria, and to the ends of the earth.[10]

As noted above Luke is not averse to using the verb translated as 'make disciples'. In Acts 14 we read of Paul and Barnabas who:

After they had proclaimed the good news to that city [Derbe] and had made many disciples they returned to Lystra, then on to Iconium and Antioch.[11]

In the New Testament there is a divinely infused passion, urgency, energy and fruitfulness about the holy habit of making disciples. There is a Spirit-filled excitement in the narratives that tell of people responding to the call to follow Jesus.

The Process of Evangelism?

The shelves of Christian bookshops and Bible colleges groan under the weight of books, courses and resources that offer explanations for the processes by which people come to be disciples of Jesus or offer themselves as means by which others can be invited to embark on the adventure of Christian discipleship. Process resources have helped many to respond to the call of Jesus over the years.

As I write this my good friend Rachel is climbing the slopes of Mount Kilimanjaro raising funds for Compassion UK. I first met Rachel when she phoned me up out of the blue to enquire about being confirmed. At that time I was thinking through running an Alpha course for the first time. So, always trying to spot an opportunity when it presents itself, I asked Rachel if she would like to be part of the Alpha group and suggested that when we had done the course we could discuss confirmation. Rachel agreed and Alpha proved to be a life-changing experience for her. She says,

'Alpha was hugely transformational for me, learning about who Jesus was and being given the opportunity to ask questions was a much needed step in my journey to faith. It's shaped both me and my ministry, as I've discovered that life as a Christian is an adventure, with valleys and mountain highs. I've continued on the journey with a heart that is eager and open to explore.'

On her adventure of discipleship Rachel has, amongst other things, produced programmes for BBC Radio 4, worked for Next, the Methodist Church and Fresh Expressions (with whom she hosted a day with the Archbishop of Canterbury at Holy Trinity Brompton). She has begun many initiatives within her ministry with children and families, including Maker Baker and Special Spirits (a holiday club for families with additional needs in a Christian environment). She has introduced many others to Jesus and is now climbing the highest mountain in Africa.

So process courses can and do work. The best ones (including Alpha) blend together many of the holy habits including biblical teaching, fellowship, breaking of bread, prayer, eating together, gladness and generosity and worship. So the formative learning is experiential as well as cerebral. Discipleship is caught as well as taught.

Bless, Belong, Believe

One helpful insight that has come to the fore in recent years is a renewed emphasis on the place of blessing in living out the commission to make disciples. In his inspiring booklet *Give Me a Drink* Ian Adams says this:

> I would love to see the mission of the Christ's people increasingly focus on blessing. Blessing works. I don't fully understand how or why, but I believe that it does! Perhaps in part because in blessing we are stepping consciously into the flow of God's ever creating goodness! Perhaps too because the act of blessing changes us – both blesser and receiver. We begin to perceive ourselves and the world in a different way. And perhaps too because in a world that can seem so ungracious, whenever the gift of Jesus the Christ is offered, full of grace and truth, we cannot help but be transformed, blessing by blessing! Blessing is intimately linked to the possibility of abundance. Jesus spoke of his coming to bring abundant life. Whenever the people of Jesus come tenderly offering abundance in their hands and blessing on their lips the world of deficit, cuts, shortage and austerity may begin to change for good. Whenever the people of Jesus come tenderly offering abundance in their hands and blessing on their lips the world of competing ideologies, tribes, nations and religions will begin to find more reasons to connect than disconnect. Whenever the people of Jesus come tenderly offering abundance in their hands and blessing on their lips your street, your school and your work will begin to find their healing. So how, even with limited resources, can you offer blessing and carry abundance?[12]

As we live gladly and generously blessing others, serving, sharing life and food, so the opportunities come to invite people to experience the *koinonia* of belonging. In this experience of welcoming community those curious or even sceptical can begin to explore the person, teaching and call of Jesus. As their sense of being at home or belonging grows so belief forms and commitment comes.

Markers and Milestones

In Chapter 2 we explored the stories of the calling of the first disciples of Jesus. Simon Peter's story is particularly interesting and it is an intriguing question as to when he became a disciple of Jesus. Was it at the lakeside?[13] Or was it perhaps earlier when Jesus cured his mother-in-law?[14] As the adventure of discipleship unfolds for Peter there are other milestone moments. His confession of Jesus as the Messiah.[15] His restoration by the risen Jesus following his denial which poignantly ends with Jesus reiterating the call to discipleship, 'Follow me.'[16] Then there is his participation in the outpouring of the Spirit at Pentecost[17] and the critical 'conversion' moment when he realises that God loves Gentiles too.[18]

For all those who follow Jesus on the adventure of discipleship there will be significant moments. Every journey will be unique but over time the community of disciples we call the church has come to recognise, mark and celebrate these in a number of ways.

In the early church there were two key markers towards the beginning of the journey: baptism in water and baptism in the Spirit. These were closely linked to 'conversion' or a first decision to follow Jesus.[19] Incidentally, linking to our thinking on the importance of families and homes as holy habitats in Chapter 6, it is intriguing to note how the promise of forgiveness and the gift of the Spirit is made by Peter to those who were listening, their children and for all who are far away.[20]

Today different parts of the body of Christ mark the beginning of the journey in different ways. Baptism in particular is celebrated in a range of customs and practices. There are those who believe a conscious profession of repentance, faith and desire to follow Jesus must be made by the person being baptised. There is a very clear outworking here of

Matthew 28:19 and the related commands of Jesus to make disciples, baptise and teach. Others take seriously the place of the household in the New Testament (in the book of Acts in particular[21]) and baptise the children of Christian households. There is then a service of confirmation for those who were baptised as children and want as adults to publicly profess their commitment to follow Jesus.

Peter's story encourages us to think creatively about the services and markers that are offered on the adventure of discipleship. Some traditions do offer services to mark restorative moments for those who like Peter have in some way denied or drifted away from Jesus and want to re-declare their allegiance to him. Many offer services at Easter time in which people can renew their baptismal vows. Others (not just Methodists) use the Covenant Service introduced by John Wesley as an annual renewal of their commitment to following Jesus.

An Expectation of Growth

Sadly, in recent years, when it comes to making disciples many in the Western church have bought into a narrative of decline and have limited or no expectations of making more disciples. I once got a 'parking ticket' on my car in a church car park. The church steward didn't recognise my car and assumed it belonged to a nearby resident who had forgotten to move it before the service. He never thought I might have been a visitor ...

This is a long way from the picture of the holy habitats of the early church presented by Luke in Acts 'where the Lord added to their number daily those who were being saved'.[22] Loveday Alexander points out[23] that growth is constantly highlighted in Acts.[24] There is:

- Numerical growth.[25]
- Geographical expansion.[26]
- Growth in ethnic diversity.[27]

Happily there are many today who do have the kind of fervour depicted by Luke in Acts and are expecting and seeing growth in Christian community and the number of disciples being made. In the UK many of these are newer churches, fresh expressions of church,

Pentecostal churches and black majority churches.[28]

Through her ministry as an evangelism enabler Elaine Lindridge has encouraged the growth of many Christian communities. When leading Mind the Gap in Gateshead, a Fresh Expression that we encountered earlier in Norma's story, Elaine unashamedly said:

> We *expect* to grow. We *expect* new people to join. We *expect* to get bigger and multiply.[29]

Around the world the growth in the number of those following Jesus is expanding rapidly, especially in Africa, Latin America and South-East Asia. In November 2014 *The Economist* published a fascinating article on the growth of Christianity in China. It reported that:

> Christianity is hard to control in China, and getting harder all the time. It is spreading rapidly, and infiltrating the party's own ranks.
>
> Many experts, foreign and Chinese, now accept that there are probably more Christians than there are members of the 87 million strong Communist Party.
>
> In the 1980s the faith grew most quickly in the countryside, stimulated by the collapse of local health care and a belief that Christianity could heal instead. In recent years it has been burgeoning in cities.
>
> Some Chinese also discern in Christianity the force behind the development of social justice, civil society and rule of law, all things they hope to see in China.
>
> In [some] regions local leaders lend support, or turn a blind eye, because they find that Christians are good citizens. Their commitment to community welfare helps to reinforce precious stability.[30]

The picture *The Economist* paints is not that dissimilar to the portrait of growth that Luke presents in Acts. The rapid growth of the Jesus movement enjoying the goodwill of the people. Should we be surprised? Not if we believe that the same Jesus who said 'I will build my church'[31] you 'go and make disciples'[32] and you will be 'clothed with power from on high'[33] knew what he was on about.

Suggestions for Further Reflection and Action

Personally
To whom could you be a blessing today?

If a strange car appeared on your church car park what would you do?

Locally
Within the Great Commission there is the command to go (and make disciples). To whom do you sense a call to go to be a blessing and share the invitation to explore the call of Jesus to follow? Are there any people groups in your community that you feel a particular calling to?

How could you blend the holy habits to offer a space in which people could explore the call of Jesus?

Globally
Discover more of how disciples of Jesus are being made around the world. Organisations like CMS (cms-uk.org) or Operation World (operationworld.org) can be very helpful here.

Partner with and be inspired by a growing fellowship from another part of the world.

Pray for and support those in countries where making new disciples of Jesus would be dangerous or illegal. The Open Doors website provides valuable information for prayer: opendoorsuk.org.

A Biblical Passage to Reflect On
• Matthew 28:16–20

What do you notice in this passage?

What will you do or change in the light of what you have read and noticed?

Recommended Reading
• Mike Booker and Mark Ireland, *Making New Disciples: Exploring the Paradoxes of Evangelism*
• Steven Croft, Rob Frost, Mark Ireland, Anne Richards, Yvonne

Richmond and Nick Spencer, *Evangelism in a Spiritual Age.*

• Steve Hollingurst, *Mission Shaped Evangelism.*

Endnotes

1. David Watson, *Discipleship*, London: Hodder and Stoughton, 1981, p37.

2. freshexpressions.org.uk/stories/grafted/luke.

3. Steve Hollinghurst, *Mission Shaped Evangelism*, Norwich: Canterbury Press, 2010, p248.

4. Ibid, p249.

5. Ibid, p248.

6. Matthew28:19–20a.

7. Matthew 13:52; 28:19–20 and Acts 14:1.

8. Steven Croft, *Jesus the Evangelist (according to Matthew)*, Address to the Fellowship of Parish Evangelists, January 2007.

9. Matthew 28:19–20.

10. Acts 1:8.

11. Acts 14:21.

12. Ian Adams, *Give Me a Drink*, proost.co.uk, 2015, p22.

13. Luke 5:1–11.

14. Luke 4:38–39.

15. Luke 9:20.

16. John 21:19.

17. Acts 2.

18. Acts 10.

19. Acts 2:37–41.

20. Acts 2:39.

21. See for example Acts 2:39 and Peter's words that the promise of forgiveness and the Spirit is for you [and] for your children.

22. Acts 2:47.

23. Loveday Alexander, 'What patterns of church and mission are found in the Acts of the Apostles?' in S. Croft (ed), *Mission Shaped Questions*, London: Church House Publishing, 2008, p133.

24. Acts 6:7; 12:24; 19:20.

25. Acts 2:41; 4:4.

26. Acts 1:8; 8:25; 9:31; 11:19–20; chapters 13 – 20, 27 – 28.

27. Acts 8:27; 10:1ff; 11:18,20; 13:46–48; 14:11; 18:6; 28:4; 28:28.

28. For more on this see David Goodhew, *Church Growth in Britain*, Farnham: Ashgate, 2012.

29. Norman Ivison, *expressions: the dvd – 1: stories of church for a changing culture*, London: Church House Publishing, 2006, Ch 15. Or freshexpressions.org.uk/resources/dvd1/15.

30. economist.com/news/briefing/21629218-rapid-spread-christianity-forcing-official-rethink-religion-cracks.

31. Matthew 16:18.

32. Matthew 28:19.

33. Luke 24:49.

18

Dare to Dream

In the last days it will be, God declares,
that I will pour out my Spirit upon all flesh,
and your sons and your daughters shall prophesy,
and your young men shall see visions,
and your old men shall dream dreams.
Acts 2:17

Einstein once said that what you can't imagine you will never see. One of the gifts of the Spirit that is being rediscovered in these days is that of prophetic imagination. As our look at ten holy habits draws to a close, I invite you to explore that gift for a moment and dare to dream.

When the Spirit was poured out at Pentecost, fulfilling the ancient prophecy of Joel, there was a release of energy, creativity and imagination. Younger people were fired with new Kingdom vision. Older people were renewed by dreams of what could be. A movement that just a few weeks before had seemed to die on a dark Friday afternoon was on fire with life, joy and a fresh belief in what was possible.

When I was writing this book I visited friends who live in Portland,

Dorset. They live near to the waters that were used for sailing and windsurfing at the 2012 Olympics. As I drove back across the causeway to the mainland I found myself being overtaken by a windsurfer skilfully catching the power of the wind in his sails. I checked my speedometer and saw that I was doing 50 mph. Which meant he was doing more . . .

Oh that we might catch again the wind of the Spirit as that windsurfer caught the wind blowing across the water that day. Oh that we might be fired with fresh imagination, dreams and vision of how the world could be if the adventure of following Jesus was lived more fully in these days.

We live in a beautiful world with dark shadows, a world of plenty but with too much poverty, a world with glimpses of heaven and ghettos of hell, a world that has never been so connected or so lonely. I invite you to dream of how this world could be if you and the communities of which you are part lived more fully the adventure of following Jesus and the holy habits of discipleship. Imagine how your world, your home, your place of work, your neighbourhood could be if daily life revolved around giving not getting, serving not selfish ambition, gladness and generosity rather than bitterness and envy.

Dream, imagine, what the world would be like if the holy habits we have been exploring were lived more fully through you, me and others adventuring in discipleship today. Imagine what signs of the Kingdom we would see. Imagine what wonders would be done.

Imagine your home, your street, your place of work, the world living by biblical teaching out of which God is honoured, creation is cared for, strangers become friends. Imagine a world where truth and goodness prevail. Where people, asking what the Lord requires of us, do justice, love kindness, and walk humbly with God.[1]

Imagine fellowship being welcoming and deep, warm and challenging, supportive and transforming. Mini Kingdom communities that fulfil the promise of Jesus: 'By this everyone will know that you are my disciples, if you have love for one another.'[2] Communities that counter the twenty-first-century epidemic of loneliness and build up the body of Christ. Holy communities that heal and make whole.

Imagine the feeding of the 5000 being re-enacted every day as bread is broken and shared on park benches, in the market place, at the roadside. Imagine the presence of Jesus being revealed when bread is blessed and broken as companions walk together, as housebound saints invite their neighbours round, as Messy kids offer bread to their parents and carers. Imagine creative celebrations of the Lord's Supper that renew the worshipping community and send out missionary disciples full of love and purpose.

Imagine prayer becoming as natural as breathing. Imagine a prayerful way of life transforming your vision so that you see glimpses of God all around, the sacred in the secular, the potential for good. Imagine your staffroom, shop floor, boardroom or changing room being touched by the holiness of the prayers you pray. Imagine prayer transcending tribes and cultures, breaking down walls and barriers, paving the pathway to a just and peaceful world.

Imagine your home, your street, your place of work, the world being keener to give than to get. Where what is mine is yours if you need it. Imagine a church known more for giving than asking – and imagine the queue at the door! Imagine more children finding loving homes, more lonely elderly people enjoying the companionship of a weekly visit from a neighbour. Imagine the millennial goals being realised as richer nations remodel unjust systems. Imagine the day when poverty is over.

Imagine the promise of Deuteronomy 15:4 being fulfilled again with no one in need among you. Imagine people campaigning and voting for the interests of others rather than seeking to preserve and protect their own interests. Imagine church buildings open 24/7 in service of the community where the words 'All are welcome' are really true. Imagine bosses kneeling at the feet of their staff literally or metaphorically to serve those they lead, valuing them as equals.

Imagine banquets and parties of good food and drink. Imagine newcomers to the neighbourhood being invited to a meal and made to feel welcome. Imagine families eating together around a table, sharing stories, saying grace, taking their time. Imagine different ethnicities and cultures finding joy and delight in tasting each other's signature dishes. Imagine the day when there will be a harvest for the world and a harvest supper for all.

Imagine a world, a church, where gladness prevails and cynicism is banished! Imagine the sight of smiles and the sound of laughter, the warmth of hugs and tears of joy as people are generous with their compliments and thanks. Imagine communities of affirmation and appreciation where gifts are honoured and celebrated, not envied. Imagine younger people generously giving time to care for older people. And imagine older people generously saying to younger people, you lead us into the future.

Imagine the whole of life being offered in worship. God being glorified in the harvesting of the crop, the styling of the hair, the satellite being launched. Imagine gatherings for worship bursting with creativity that do lead to people being lost in wonder, love and praise. Imagine worship that brings the hurts of the world to the heart of God and that inspires the worshippers to go out and touch that world with holy, healing hands.

And imagine how things would be if more disciples were made day by day to live out these holy transformational habits. If every disciple of Jesus invited just one other to 'come and see', to come and find out more about the one who loves them, died and rose for them and longs to give them life in all its fullness.

Crazy? Ridiculous? Well so was a bunch of fishermen leaving their nets to follow a young wandering rabbi embarking on what became a life-changing, world-transforming holy adventure.

Just a dream? Well so was Martin Luther King's dream that 'one day right here in Alabama little black boys and black girls will be able to join hands with little white boys and white girls as sisters and brothers'. But it came true.

Impossible? Well so was the idea that a dying chapel in Yorkshire could ever be full to overflowing again with the sound of children's laughter filling the air, baptisms in ball pools and fully subscribed Alpha courses. But it happened.

Pious nonsense? Well not for a young lady, Julie, who fell through the door of Zac's Place in Swansea f-ing and blinding, in a total mess. One of the Zaclicans sat her down whilst others prayed and another took a bowl and towel and started to gently wash her feet. As the water and prayers washed over her so her demeanour changed and this angry and hurting young woman began to relax and smile and quietly sing 'Jesus loves me this I know for the Bible tells me so'. Heaven and earth touched. Julie died just a few days later. Her father asked that they sang 'Jesus loves me' at the funeral. 'So you know what happened when she visited us,' Pastor Sean said. 'No,' the father replied. 'That was the song Julie's mother used to sing to her as she rocked her to sleep.'[3]

Holy Simplicity

The holy habits are not complicated. They can be lived out as simply as by providing a chair and a bowl of water. They are a way of life to be lived. Love in action. Embodied grace.

To practise them we don't need a PhD, just a willingness to follow Jesus. We don't need a church building – although practising them there is a good idea! Like a glass of Martini they can be offered and enjoyed anytime, anyplace, anywhere. In villages, towns and cities. Any context, culture, community or country. We can be 5, 95 or any age in between or either side. So I invite you to give them a fresh go.

As you do so don't forget the holy part of holy habits. On the adventure of discipleship we are called to holiness. 'Be holy because I am holy,'[4] says the Lord. So being holy involves being close to, intimate with, the divine community of Father, Son and Holy Spirit.

So keep close to the Father. Let the Father's creativity infuse the habits as you practise them. Let there be colour and variety, freshness and vitality. Let the Father's generous giving of creation, of love, of salvation, shape you. Let the Father's passion for the poor and thirst for justice and righteousness inform and guide you.

Keep close to the Son, the one who calls you and through you calls others to follow on the adventure of discipleship. Let the mind of the Son 'dwell in you richly'.[5] Let the resolve and self-giving, sacrificial love of the Son be your model for living. Let the incarnate, down-to-earth, involved way of life of the Son keep you grounded and immersed in the joys and struggles, laughter and tears of life. And enjoy the parties and banquets, the laughter of children, the tender touches of love and the joys of creation the Son enjoyed when walking this earth.

And keep on being filled with the life-giving, God-breathing, flame-warming Spirit.[6] Let the fruits of love, joy, peace, patience, kindness, generosity, faithfulness, gentleness, and self-control flavour your practising of the holy habits.[7] Pray for the gifts of the Spirit to be released afresh in you and amongst those you live the adventure of discipleship with. Let the Spirit inspire new dreams and visions of how you can be part of the Kingdom coming in and through your home, church, community, workplace, world.

Follow Me

'Follow me,' says Jesus. Two simple yet life-changing, world-changing, words. Dare to dream what you can be and do, as renewed by the Spirit you follow afresh the one who loves you, calls you and walks with you. Dare to dream of how your home, church, community, workplace, world can be transformed as you live out the holy habits in partnership with the Holy Community of Father, Son and Holy Spirit.

'Follow me,' says Jesus. It's time to take the next step.

Endnotes

1. Micah 6:8.
2. John 13:35.
3. Norman Ivison, *expressions: making a difference,* Fresh Expressions, 2011, Ch 28. Or freshexpressions.org.uk/resources/makingadifference/28.
4. Leviticus 11:45.
5. Colossians 3:16.
6. Ephesians 5:18.
7. Galatians 5:22–23.

Bibliography

Commentaries and Articles on Acts and the Gospels

Acts

Alexander, Loveday, *Acts: The People's Bible Commentary*, Oxford: Bible Reading Fellowship, 2006.

Barrett, C.K., *Acts 1–14, ICC*, Edinburgh: T&T Clark, 2004.

Blue, Bradley, *Acts and the House Church* in Gill, D.W.J. and Gempf, C. (eds), *The Book of Acts in its First Century Setting*, Carlisle: Paternoster Press, 1994.

Bruce, F.F., *The Book of the Acts Revised*, Grand Rapids: Eerdmans, 1988.

Conzelmann, H., *The Acts of the Apostles*, Philadelphia: Fortress, 1987.

Dunn, James D.G., *The Acts of the Apostles*, Peterborough: Epworth, 1996.

Haenchen, E., *The Acts of the Apostles*, Oxford: Basil Blackwell, 1971.

Marshall, I. Howard, *Acts*, Leicester: Inter-Varsity Press, 1980.

Roberts, Andrew, *The Acts of the Apostles; Resourcing and Developing Fresh Expressions of Church* in Epworth Review: Volume 36, Number 3, London: Trustees for Methodist Church Purposes, July 2009.

Stott, John R.W., *The Message of Acts*, Leicester: IVP, 1990.

Willimon, W.H., *Interpretation of Acts*, Atlanta: John Knox Press 1988.

Wittherington, Ben, *The Acts of the Apostles: a Socio-Rhetorical Commentary*, Grand Rapids: Eerdmans, 1988.

Yao, Santos, 'Dismantling Social Barriers Through Table Fellowship' in Gallagher, R.L. and Hertig, P., *Mission in Acts*, New York: Orbis, 2004.

Matthew

Croft, Steven, *Jesus the Evangelist (according to Matthew)*, Address to the Fellowship of Parish Evangelists, January 2007.

Davies, W. D. and Allison, D. C., *International Critical Commentary Matthew Volume III*, Edinburgh, T&T Clark, 1997.

Mark

English, Donald, *The Message of Acts*, Leicester: IVP, 1992.

Guelich, Robert A., *Mark 1 – 8:26, Word Biblical Commentary 34a*, Dallas: Word Books, 1989.

Hooker, Morna D., *The Gospel According to St Mark*, London: Black's, 1991.

Lane, William L., *The Gospel of Mark*, Cambridge: Eerdmans, 1974.

Luke

Green, Joel, *The Gospel of Luke*, Cambridge: Eerdmans, 1997.

Marshall, I. Howard, *The Gospel of Luke*, Exeter: Paternoster Press, 1978.

Nolland, John, *Luke 1 – 9:20, Word Biblical Commentary 35a*, Dallas: Word Books, 1989.

Talbert, Charles H., *Reading Luke*, Macon: Smyth & Helwys, 2002.

Wright, Tom, *Luke for Everyone*, London: SPCK, 2001.

John

Barrett, C. K., *The Gospel According to St John (Second Edition)*, London: SPCK, 1978.

Beasley-Murray, George R., John, *Second Edition Word Biblical Commentary 36*, Mexico City: Word Books, 2000.

Brown, Raymond, *The Gospel According to John (Volume 1)*, London: Geoffrey Chapman, 1966.

Hylen, Susan E., *Imperfect Believers, Ambiguous Characters in the Gospel of John*, Louisville: John Knox Press, 2009.

Köstenberger, Andreas J., *The Mission of Jesus and the Disciples According to the Fourth Gospel*, Grand Rapids: Eerdmans, 1998.

Other texts

Adams, Ian, *Cave, Refectory, Road*, Norwich: Canterbury Press, 2010.

Adams, Ian, *Give Me a Drink*, proost.co.uk, 2015.

Adams, Ian, *Running Over Rocks*, Norwich: Canterbury Press, 2013.

Aldrin, Buzz, *Magnificent Desolation*, London: Bloomsbury, 2009.

Atkins, Martyn, *Discipleship and the People Called Methodists*, Peterborough: Trustees for Methodist Church Purposes, 2010.

Baker, Dilly, *Liturgies and Resources for Christ-centred Hospitality*, Norwich: Canterbury Press, 2008.

Baker, Jonny, *Curating Worship*, London: SPCK, 2010.

Baker, Jonny and Ross, Cathy (eds), *The Pioneer Gift*, London: Canterbury Press, 2014.

Bhogal, Inderjit, *A Table For All: A Challenge to Church and Nation*. Penistone: Penistone Publications, 2000.

Bonhoeffer, Dietrich, *Letters and Papers from Prison*, London: SCM Press, 2001.

Bonhoeffer, Dietrich, *Life Together*, London: SCM, 1954.

Bonhoeffer, Dietrich, *The Cost of Discipleship*, London: SCM Press, 2001.

Booker, Mike and Ireland, Mark, *Making New Disciples: Exploring the Paradoxes of Evangelism*. London: SPCK, 2015.

Bramley, John, *Remember Who You Represent*, Sandy: Authors on Line, 2009.

Brueggemann, Walter, *The Word That Redescribes the World*, Minneapolis: Fortress Press, 2006.

Cassidy, Sheila, *Sharing the Darkness*, London: Darton, Longman and Todd, 1988.

Cassidy, Sheila, *Good Friday People*, London: Darton, Longman and Todd, 1991.

Coffey, Ian, *Pennies for Heaven*, Eastbourne: Kingsway, 1984.

Cray, Graham, *Disciples and Citizens*, Nottingham: IVP, 2007.

Cray, Graham, Mobsby, Ian and Kennedy, Aaron, *New Monasticism as Fresh Expression of Church*, Norwich: Canterbury Press, 2010.

Cray, Graham, Mobsby, Ian and Kennedy, Aaron, *Fresh Expression of Church and the Kingdom of God*, Norwich: Canterbury Press, 2012.

Croft, Steven, Frost, Rob, Ireland, Mark, Richards, Anne, Richmond, Yvonne and Spencer, Nick, *Evangelism in a Spiritual Age*, London: Church House Publishing, 2005.

Croft, Steven, *Growing New Christians*, London: Marshall Pickering,

1993.

Croft, Steven, Jesus' People: *What the Church Should Do Next*, London: Church House Publishing, 2009.

Croft, Steven (ed), *Mission Shaped Questions*, London: Church House Publishing, 2008.

Drane, John, *Introducing the New Testament* (Third Edition), Oxford: Lion, 2010.

Dunn, James D.G., *Jesus and the Spirit*, London: SCM Press, 1975.

Foster, Richard, *Celebration of Discipline*, London: Hodder and Stoughton, 1989.

Freeman, Andy and Greig, Pete, *Punk Monk*, Eastbourne: Kingsway, 2007.

Glasson, Barbara, *Mixed-up Blessing*, Peterborough: Inspire, 2006.

Glasson, Barbara, *I Am Somewhere Else*, London: Darton, Longman and Todd, 2006.

Gooder, Paula, *Everyday God*, Norwich: Canterbury Press, 2012.

Gooder, Paula, *Heaven*, London: SPCK, 2011.

Goodhew, David, Roberts, Andrew and Volland, Michael, *fresh! An Introduction to Fresh Expressions of Church and Pioneer Ministry*, London: SCM Press, 2012.

Gray-Reeves, Mary and Perham, Michael, *The Hospitality of God*, London: SPCK, 2011.

Greig, Pete, *The Vision and the Vow*, Eastbourne: Kingsway, 2005.

Greig, Pete, *God on Mute*, Eastbourne: Kingsway, 2007.

Greene, Mark, *Fruitfulness on the Frontline*, Nottingham: IVP, 2014.

Guillebaud, Simon, *More Than Conquerors*, Oxford: Monarch Books, 2009.

Hart, Sylvia, *Extending the Table, A World Community, Cookbook, Friends, Faith and Feasts*, Peterborough: Inspire, 2006.

Hawking, Jane, *Travelling to Infinity*, Richmond: Alma Books, 2008.

Henderson, Michael, *Forgiveness: Breaking the Chain of Hate*, London: Grosvenor Books, 2002.

Hirst, Judy, *Struggling to be Holy*, London: Darton, Longman and Todd, 2008.

Hollinghurst, Steve, *Mission Shaped Evangelism*, Norwich: Canterbury Press, 2010.

Hooker, Morna D., *Beginnings: Keys that Open the Gospels*, London: SCM, 1997.

Hooker, Morna D., *Endings: Invitations to Discipleship*, London: SCM, 2003.

Hooker, Morna D. and Young, Francis, *Holiness and Mission*, London: SCM, 2010.

Hull, John M., *Mission Shaped Church: A Theological Response*, London: SCM, 2006.

Ilibagiza, Immaculée, *Left to Tell*, London: Hay House, 2007.

Johnson, Peter and Sugden, Chris (eds), *Markets, Fair Trade and the Kingdom of God*, Oxford: Regnum, 2001.

Keating, Charles J., *Who We Are is How We Pray*, Mystic: Twenty-Third Publications, 2004.

Kendrick, Graham, *Worship*, Eastbourne: Kingsway, 1984.

Lawrence, Louise, *The Word in Place*, London: SPCK, 2009.

Milne, Bruce, *Know the Truth*, Leicester: IVP, 1982.

Mobsby Ian and Berry, Mark, *A New Monastic Handbook*, Norwich: Canterbury Press, 2014.

Moore, Paul, *Making Disciples in Messy Church*, Abingdon: Bible Reading Fellowship, 2013.

Morgan, Alison, *The Wild Gospel*, Abingdon: Monarch Books, 2004.

Morgan, Alison, *Following Jesus: The Plural of Disciple is Church*, Wells; Resource, 2015.

Morisy, Ann, *Journeying Out*, London: Continuum, 2004.

Moynagh, Michael, *Being Church, Doing Life*, Oxford: Monarch Books, 2014.

Muamba, Fabrice, *I'm Still Standing*, Liverpool: Sport Media, 2012.

Ortberg, John, *If You Want to Walk on Water, You've Got to Get Out of the Boat*, Grand Rapids: Zondervan, 2001.

Peppiatt, Lucy, *The Disciple*, Eugene: Cascade, 2012.

Prior, David, *The Church in the Home*, Basingstoke: Marshall, Morgan and Scott, 1983.

Pullin, Tony, *Making Disciples*, Farnham: CWR, 2014.

Regis, Cyrille, *Cyrille Regis My Story*, London: Andre Deutsch, 2010.

Shier-Jones, Angela, *Pioneer Ministry and Fresh Expressions of Church*, London: SPCK, 2009.

Smith, James K.A., *Desiring the Kingdom: Worship, Worldview, and Cultural Formation*, Grand Rapids: Baker Academic, 2009.

Stockman, Steve, *Walk On: The Spiritual Journey of U2*, Orlando: Relevant Media, 2005.

Stoddard, Chris and Cuthbert, Nick, *Church on the Edge*, Milton Keynes: Authentic Media, 2006.

Stott, John R.W., *Christian Mission in the Modern World*, London: CPAS, 1975.

Sweet, Leonard, *From Tablet to Table*, NavPress, 2014.

The Methodist Church, *His Presence Makes the Feast*, Peterborough, TMCP, 2006.

Tomlin, Graham, *Spiritual Fitness*, London: Continuum, 2006.

Vanier, Jean, *Community and Growth*, London: Darton, Longman and Todd, 1980.

Waite, Terry, *Taken on Trust*, London: Hodder and Stoughton, 1993.

Wallace, Sue, *Multi-sensory Prayer*, Bletchley: Scripture Union, 2007.

Wallace, Sue, *Multi-sensory Scripture*, Bletchley: Scripture Union, 2005.

Wallace, Sue, *Multi-sensory Worship*, Bletchley: Scripture Union, 2009.

Wallis, Jim, *On God's Side: What Religion Forgets and Politics Hasn't Learned About Serving the Common Good*, Grand Rapids: Brazos Press, 2013.

Warren, Robert, *Developing Healthy Churches*, London: Church House Publishing, 2012.

Walton, Roger L., *Disciples Together*, London: SCM Press, 2014.

Walton, Roger L., *The Reflective Disciple*, London: SCM Press, 2012.

Watson, David, *Discipleship*, London: Hodder and Stoughton, 1981.

Watson, David, *Fear No Evil*, London: Hodder and Stoughton, 1984.

Wicks, Robert J., *Everday Simplicity: A Practical Guide to Spiritual Growth*, Notre Dame: Sorin Books, 2000.

Wicks, Robert J., *Touching the Holy*, Notre Dame: ave maria press, 2004.

Wilkey-Collinson, Sylvia, *Making Disciples*, Milton Keynes: Paternoster, 2004.

Wilkinson, David, *When I Pray What Does God Actually Do?*, Oxford: Monarch Books, 2015.

Wimber, John, *Power Evangelism*, London: Hodder and Stoughton, 2001.

Witherington, Ben, *Jesus and Money*, London: SPCK, 2010.

Yancey, Philip, *What's So Amazing About Grace?* Grand Rapids: Zondervan, 1997.

Websites/pages

24-7prayer.com/communities/practices

archbishopofcanterbury.org/articles.php/5515/lambeth-lectures-archbishop-justin-on-evangelism-video

bbc.co.uk/sport/0/football/34261682

Biblesociety.org.uk/about-Bible-society/our-work/lyfe/what-is-lyfe/

freshexpressions.org.uk

godlyplay.uk

hobstafford.co.uk/bread-church

licc.org.uk/imagine-church

lindisfarne-scriptorium.co.uk

messychurch.org.uk

methodist.org.uk/media/636034/venturefx-rhythm-of-life-0912.pdf

methodist.org.uk/media/831306/dd-explore-devotion-writing-a-rule-of-life-0313.pdf

somewhere-else.org.uk

DVDs

Ivison, Norman, *expressions: the dvd – 1: stories of church for a changing culture*, London: Church House Publishing, 2006.

Ivison, Norman, *expressions: making a difference*, Fresh Expressions, 2011.